MUHAMMAD
ALL THAT MATTERS

About the author

Ziauddin Sardar, writer, broadcaster and cultural critic, is Professor of Law and Society at Middlesex University. Considered a pioneering writer on Islam and contemporary cultural issues, he is author of some 50 books and co-editor of the quarterly *Critical Muslim*.

His books include *The Future of Muslim Civilisation* (1979), *Islamic Futures: The Shape of Ideas to Come* (1985), *Postmodernism and the Other* (1998), *Orientalism* (1999), the international bestseller *Why Do People Hate America?* (2002) and *Reading the Qur'an* (2011). He has also published two volumes of autobiography, *Desperately Seeking Paradise: Journeys of a Sceptical Muslim* (2004) and *Balti Britain: A Provocative Journey Through Asian Britain* (2008). A collection of his writings is available as *Islam, Postmodernism and Other Futures: A Ziauddin Sardar Reader* (2003) and *How Do You Know? Reading Ziauddin Sardar on Islam, Science and Cultural Relations* (2006). He is widely known as a public intellectual and appears frequently on radio and television.

MUHAMMAD

Ziauddin Sardar

ALL THAT MATTERS

ALL THAT MATTERS

Hodder Education
338 Euston Road, London NW1 3BH.

Hodder Education is an Hachette UK company

First published in UK 2012 by Hodder Education

First published in US 2012 by The McGraw-Hill Companies, Inc.

This edition published 2012

British Library Cataloguing in Publication Data: a catalogue record for this title is available from the British Library.

Library of Congress Catalog Card Number: on file.

10 9 8 7 6 5 4 3 2

www.hoddereducation.co.uk

Typeset by Cenveo Publisher Services.

Printed in Great Britain by CPI Group (UK) Ltd, Croydon, CR0 4YY.

Contents

Acknowledgements

The author and publishers would like to thank the following for their permission to reproduce photos in this book. **Chapter 3:** © ayazad – Fotolia; **Chapter 4:** Walters Art Museum/http://creativecommons.org/licenses/by-sa/3.0/deed.en 28/03/2012/http://commons.wikimedia.org/wiki/File:Turkish_-_Tile_with_the_Great_Mosque_of_Mecca_-_Walters_481307_-_View_A.jpg; **Chapter 5:** http://en.wikipedia.org/wiki/File:Cave_Hira.jpg (Nazli – public domain); **Chapter 6:** © Ahmad Faizal Yahya – Fotolia; **Chapter 7:** © Ahmad Faizal Yahya – Fotolia; **Chapter 9:** http://en.wikipedia.org/wiki/File:Sana%27_military_museum_07.JPG (public domain); **Chapter 11:** © ramzi hachicho – Fotolia.

Understanding Muhammad

ALL THAT
MATTERS

Prophets are persons of renown. The greatest of them – Abraham, Moses, Buddha, Jesus, Muhammad – have indisputably changed the course of human history. They have reshaped the daily lives of ordinary people and the societies in which they lived and altered people's relationship to the world around them and to history. How we know and think about ourselves, life, the world and everything today bears the hallmarks of what these prophets and their followers have thought, said and done over the course of centuries, just as in our diverse ways we have all been influenced by the reaction of their critics, sceptics, interpreters and opponents.

It would also be fair to say that while the greatest prophets have been seminal, constructive forces in human history they have also become divisive figures. As the instigators of new religious and social identities, though that might not be their intent, prophets have in effect redrawn the dividing lines, whether theological, political, social or imperial, between people. Through the varied identities their followers have constructed, battle lines have been drawn over which much blood has been spilled. Prophets inspire great love, but at times they are also used to marshal animosity and enmity. In short, prophets are inescapable figures whom we need to know and understand to make sense of human history and contemporary society.

Yet the simple fact is that in many ways prophets can be extremely difficult to know. Their biographies are encrusted with centuries of other people's ideas, prejudices and predilections. Prophets are the stuff of ideology, complicated theological reasoning, ethos, myths and legends, subjects of veneration or excoriation, most of which has less to do with the detail of their lives and deeds than with how other people want those details to be understood, accepted or rejected. Even the idea of what a prophet should ideally be like, what kind of life he should lead and what his message should contain excite different expectations depending on the conventions and beliefs with which one begins. The inevitable question arises: how is it possible to know who a prophet actually was?

Muhammad was born in Mecca, a city in what is today the country of Saudi Arabia, in the year AD 570. In his fortieth year he declared that he had received a revelation from the One God, the Creator of all that is. Until his death 23 years later, in the year 632, Muhammad was a prophet who proclaimed the revelations he continued to receive. He gathered followers, known as Muslims, people who accepted his revelations as divine and submitted to the worship of the One God, in Arabic Allah, literally meaning 'the God'. Muhammad was crucial in instituting and organizing how the religion he preached, known as Islam, was practised by his followers. These are the basic and undisputed facts, but they tell us little about Muhammad, his personality and character or the place he holds within the religion he founded.

Blessing *Salaam aly Kum*

Whenever Muslims mention the name of Muhammad, they add 'peace be upon him'. The ritual is based on a verse from the Qur'an, which states: 'God and His angels bless the Prophet – so, you who believe, bless him too and give him greetings of peace' (33: 56).

To discover more about the life and times of Muhammad is to confront a number of questions that go beyond the nature of the available evidence, the form and purpose of the historic sources. Where prophets are concerned history is not disinterested. At all times we are dealing with questions about the validity of the information derived from our sources. While this consideration is a general proposition about any kind of history, in the case of prophets the caution is redoubled. Prophets are persons who excite passionate belief on the one hand, and scepticism and even complete rejection on the other. So disputes, scholarly or otherwise, about the nature of sources will always be there.

▶ Muslim sources

However, we know more about Muhammad than any other prophet. He lived in the full light of history and there are a number of sources about his life that we can consult. First, there is the Qur'an, the collection of divine revelations, dictated and compiled under the personal supervision of Muhammad himself. The definition of a Muslim is a person who accepts and believes the Qur'an to be the direct word of God transmitted to Muhammad. During his career as a prophet, Muhammad had approximately 65 companions who functioned as his scribes.[1] As a matter of routine, when a verse was revealed, Muhammad called one of his scribes to write it down. A definitive written text of the Qur'an, from which all versions of the book extant today derive, was compiled by AD 650, some 18 years after Muhammad's death. It was put together under the auspices of his third successor as leader of the Muslim community, Caliph Uthman, who was Muhammad's son-in-law. The work was carried out by a committee of close personal companions of Muhammad who had learnt to recite the verses or had recorded them directly from the prophet.

The Qur'an contains 6,211 verses, known as *ayat*, arranged in 114 *surahs* or chapters. It is, however, not a narrative of the life of Muhammad, though it does address events in his life and in the community he gathered around him. Rather, it serves as a commentary on his life.[2] As there is a general consensus, which includes both Muslim scholars and Western critics, that the text itself remains intact, it serves as a reliable reference point about some of the main events in the life of Muhammad. One thing the Qur'an makes clear is that Muhammad is an ordinary human being, though marked out by the extraordinary call to prophethood. He is asked by the Qur'an to 'Say, "I am anything but mortal, a messenger"' (17: 93). His task is to relay the Word of God to his people and live according to its precepts; he is neither divine nor does he have the power to perform miracles – the sole miracle Islam acknowledges is the revelation of the Qur'an itself. The Qur'an also recognizes the difficulties Muhammad faced in his life and his doubts, and that as a human being he made errors.

Second, there is the huge corpus of *hadith*, sayings of Muhammad, and *Sunnah*, a record of what he did, as related by his companions.

During his own lifetime, Muhammad did not allow anything he said to be written down except the Qur'an and a couple of important legal documents.

He also wrote letters to monarchs of Abyssinia, Egypt and the Byzantine Empire, which have survived. Muhammad was born into and lived in a predominantly oral society, in which there was a strong tradition of learning by heart. As such, the Arabs preferred to memorize rather than write down things. Thus, his companions memorized his sayings when he was alive, and they were not written down till the early 700s, a task undertaken by the second generation of Muslims. To ensure that his sayings were trustworthy and authentic, Muslim scholars developed a special tool, the *isnad*, or the chain of transmitters, which traced the text, or the hadith, right back to Muhammad himself. The initial narrator of any hadith or deed of the prophet, or description of an event in his life, had to be an eyewitness to what was recounted. Moreover, detailed investigation was carried out about each narrator in the chain, his moral character, whether it was physically possible for the consecutive narrators to actually have met, and what they actually reported was reasonable or not. Then, the hadith were classified as *sahih* (authentic), *hasan* (good but with a weak chain of narrators) and *daeef* (weak with a defective chain of narrators). There were numerous other categories. Compilers of hadith critically sifted through hundreds of thousands of hadith and carefully scrutinized every single one to isolate and identify the most authentic.[3] Imam Bhkhari (810–70), who compiled the first authentic collection,[4] is said to have travelled all over Arabia, and collected around 600,000 hadith from over a thousand men. After a critical examination of his collection, he selected only 7,275 as possibly authentic. Similarly, Imam Muslim (821–75), who produced the second authentic collection,[5] selected 9,200 as authentic from a collection of 300,000. There are also other collections of hadith.

Third, there are the biographies of Muhammad, known as *sira*, that were compiled using the hadith literature. Some biographies were even prepared during the time of his companions, consisting mostly of the accounts of Muhammad's campaigns. The earliest journals of the battles, known as *maghazi*, and attributed to Urwah bin Al-Zubiar (d. 712), Muhammad bin Muslim (d. 741) and Musa bin Uqbah (d. 758), record events leading to expeditions and battles. But the first detailed biographies of Muhammad were produced by ibn Ishaq (d. 761 or 767). The original manuscripts of ibn Ishaq have survived only in fragments, but his work was preserved by his student, ibn Hasham (d. 833), who edited and combined his two books into a single volume. *The Life of Muhammad* by ibn Ishaq,[6] as edited by ibn Hisahm, is the major source of Muhammad's biography, referred to by all scholars of both the East and the West. More detailed biographies were written by later scholars, such as al-Waqidi (747–823),[7] ibn Sa'd (784–845)[8] and many others. So, unlike other prophets, we have complete biographies of Muhammad.

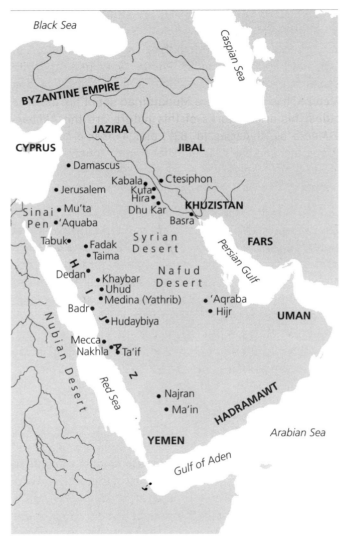

▲ Map of Arabia

Fourth, the *akhbar* (literary 'reports') are literature produced by Muslim historians. Reports of Muhammad's activities, in the form of hadith as well as testimonies of eyewitnesses to particular events, were used to write universal histories as well as annals of Mecca and Medina, two cities where Muhammad spent his life. The oldest historical works of this nature are the *Akhbar-e-Mecca* by Al-Azraqi (d. 837) and *Akhbar-e-Medina* by Umar bin Shaiba (d. 875). These were followed by the monumental universal history of al-Tabari (838–923), *History of Prophets and Kings*.[9] Such works enable us to give a wider context to the life of Muhammad.

Fifth, the poetry of the period also provides us with material about Muhammad's life. Pre-Islamic Arabia preserved its national history, and genealogical data, through poetry – not surprising for an oral society. And poetry produced by contemporary poets talks about certain events in Muhammad's life, such as his battles and his disputes with his enemies, as well as his character and dealings. This is why the early biographies of the prophet are so infused with poems – some of which are quite long!

▶ Criticism

Jesus also

There is, thus, an abundance of material about the life of Muhammad. The problem is that most of this material was produced a considerable time after his death. Generally speaking, we can divide the periods during which these sources emerged into three phases. The first phase was during Muhammad's own life when the Qur'an was revealed, his treaties and agreements were recorded and his letters were written. Then came a period when Muslim scholars and historians collected the oral material about Muhammad – this phase extended to about a hundred years after his death. The final phase, when written biographies were produced, began a hundred years after his death and continued for a couple of centuries.

Given this timescale, we can legitimately ask a number of questions about these sources. How reliable are these accounts, given that the first, ibn Ishaq's *Life of Muhammad*, was written 150 years after Muhammad's death? As hadith, which were collected anywhere between 150 and 200 years after the death of the prophet, constitute the basic raw material for sira and early Islamic history, how reliable are these eyewitness accounts? Despite the monumental efforts of Muslim scholars and the methodology of hadith criticism, it is still a human effort, prone to error and mistakes – excellent memories notwithstanding. Even if a hadith has been declared authentic, was it not possible for forgers to invent the chain of narrators – the isnad?

Muslim scholars were aware of these criticisms. Indeed, disputes about the authenticity and the role of hadith emerged right from the beginning; and opposition to hadith was not uncommon in the classical period of Islam.[10] That is why hadith criticism was not based solely on formal isnad – there were a number of other equally important criteria. For example, when a hadith was narrated the proximity to the time of Muhammad was seriously considered – the more removed the less reliable. Even when a chain of narrators was complete, the account might be unsatisfactory and rejected. Similarly, ibn Isahq, who had actually seen at least one of the companions of Muhammad, was regarded as much more reliable than other historians, such as al-Tarabi. But doubts about the authenticity of hadith remain, and there is little doubt that many hadith, even in the so-called authentic collections, are quite dubious. However, when all the limitations and criticism have been considered, one has to conclude, in the words of Reverend A Guillaume, who translated ibn Isahq into English, that the 'life of Muhammad is recorded with honesty and truthfulness and, too, an impartiality which is rare in such writings'.[11]

There is another, more recent, criticism to consider.

> *The question frequently posed by critics, especially in contemporary secular circles, is whether those who define themselves as believers can be objective.*

The sira is sacred history written by people who accepted Muhammad as a prophet and is based on certain faith claims. The question is legitimate so long as it too is subjected to critical scrutiny. To argue, for example, that we should use only non-Muslim sources to develop a picture of Muhammad's life is quite dumbfounding. To begin with, the non-Muslim sources of the seventh century provide virtually no information on Muhammad. Using these so-called sources, some Western scholars totally deny the possibility of writing a biography of Muhammad and argue that only his epoch can be described. Others have reached equally untenable conclusions, such as Muhammad did not really exist, Islam is a form of messianic Judaism and the Qur'an was produced in Syria. Some others aim to prove, with the aid of statistics and other devices, that nothing in the Muslim tradition is correct.[12] There is an old and well-established Western tradition, known as Orientalism, of denigrating sources on both Muhammad and Muslim history.[13] It has re-emerged as neo-Orientalist revisionist history, with a generous application of Islamophobia. This revisionist history has been rightly discredited. However, it is worth noting that classical Muslim scholarship is far more critical and self-reflexive than much of the contemporary, revisionist history about the origins of Islam that seeks to discredit it.

Revisionist historians

The revisionist historians, such as Patricia Crone, Michael Cook and John Wansbrough, present the origins of Islam as a massive Muslim conspiracy. Muslim historians and biographers of Muhammad manufactured the entire narrative of the seventh century, they assert. The Qur'an and the life of Muhammad were cobbled from Near Eastern religious texts and a sacred history was constructed to create a religious vision that was then anchored in the seventh century. This revisionist history has been discredited and debunked by modern scholars.

To discount all Muslim sources prima facie as partial and prejudiced is indeed to disparage not only all believers but the very concept of belief itself. To disqualify all believers as incapable of objectivity and critical method runs contrary to the clear evidence contained within the classical Muslim sources. However, it is equally clear that much of the information that comes to us about Muhammad was generated by different factions with vested interests who disputed how his example and words should be translated into law governing the practice of religion and society. There is also evidence of apocryphal stories that sought to embellish the life of the prophet of Islam; indeed, there is a whole genre of literature that ascribes miracles to Muhammad, probably influenced by the narratives of the prophets of Judaism. The challenge for modern scholarship is to sift through this extensive material critically, separating the wheat from the chaff, to arrive at viable historical truth. To reject Muslim sources wholesale makes no sense; it is a rejection based on prejudicial and political judgements.

Muslim understanding of Muhammad is not only a work of history. The prophet Muhammad is alive, intensely so, in the consciousness of all Muslims today. His personality, his words and deeds are taught to all Muslim children as if he were a living part of their daily experience. Popular aphorism based on the sayings and deeds of Muhammad are part of normal conversation. They cover the gamut from how to pray to matters of etiquette and personal hygiene, to how one should respond to the needs of the poor and weak or the labourer, to respect for parents and the importance of a love for learning. To dismiss this living tradition as entirely partial and largely mythical would be to underestimate and disparage the function of Muhammad as the exemplar of how to live a virtuous life. Also, it overlooks the fact that at all times in history and today, no matter how much embellishment and mythic material has been embroidered on to what Muslims know about Muhammad, there are always Islamic scholars who seek objective and critical insight about their prophet as a means of enriching their own understanding of faith and its practice. In all its diversity, how Muslims understand and respond to Muhammad is a necessary part of any critical and balanced enquiry.

All history is selective, picking and choosing, sifting and arranging what the author considers important, relevant, interesting or merely diverting. We can never know everything about the past any more than we know everything about the world we live in today. It is also true that historians throughout time are often partial to their own particular opinion, ideology or theory that shapes their vision and presentation of the past. There are always historians who are uncritical of their source material and others who manipulate information to serve their own agenda; equally there are historians who are critical and scrupulous as well as cautious and sceptical about what they find in their source material. All of these tendencies can be found in classical Muslim sources – as, of course, they can be found in modern Western scholarship.

In the narrative that follows, I have relied on classical Muslim sources – as indeed all contemporary biographies of Muhammad do. I have concentrated on the main events of his life for which there is considerable evidence – documents as well as written records. Of course, I have my own particular take on Muhammad as a rational, thinking individual, who, burdened with a great task, tried to fulfil his mission to the best of his capabilities. He believed in consultation, planning and strategy, and, even though he may have not known how to read or write, was highly educated by the standards of his society. He lived in a particular historic period and was a product of his time. He did not, as some Muslims seem to think, perform miracles; indeed, he went out of his way to deny any miracles ascribed to him and denounce all those who made such claims. His achievements are all products of his determination, steadfastness, compassion and a truly remarkable sense of social justice. He was a prophet, but he was also a man.

We do not have to rely on purely religious arguments to build a coherent portrait of a prophet whose life had an immense impact on history, as it does on events in today's world. We can examine the impassioned debates of Muslim scholars as well as the criticism of Western academics with an open mind and a healthy scepticism, and thus evaluate how well or ill Muhammad's followers serve his legacy. It is in this sense that we should be careful with Muhammad. It is possible to go beyond hagiography and Western stereotypes to understand Muhammad and meet a remarkable human being who made history.

2

Pre-Islamic Arabia

ALL THAT
MATTERS

To understand the evolution of Muhammad's thought, we need to appreciate the social and historical context in which he lived.

The Arabian Peninsula lies at the confluence of Asia, Africa and Europe. It is a land of mountains, desolate desert and arid regions, a harsh environment where access to water determines the pattern of life. Settled communities, towns and cities, and agriculture are possible: there are desert oases and the mountains of the southwest catch the tail of monsoon rains. The majority of the landmass, however, is scrub and desert. Around 1200 BC the domestication of the Arabian camel made possible exploitation of the most arid regions. The dominant lifestyle and economy was pastoralism – rearing animals such as camels, sheep, goats and horses. The nomadic existence varied from groups who moved seasonally between reliable grazing areas to those who were almost permanently on the move, and subsisted largely on the meat and milk and other products derived from their animals.

The nomadic pastoralists, however, did not produce all they required for subsistence; they exchanged meat, hides, milk and animals for the grain, fruits and finished goods available from the settled communities. Trade cemented relations between towns and nomads; and nomads were also supported and facilitated by shared rituals. The nomadic life required sophisticated knowledge of traversing this bleak environment and aided the opening of trade routes within and beyond Arabia. Other resources produced in Arabia, such as gold, silver and incense, were highly sought after by the advanced civilizations on its borders. Arabia was a crucial link in the global network of trade which, from antiquity, carried spices, textiles and other products from India and Ceylon by camel caravan across the Arabian deserts to the markets of the Middle East.

The Arabs were a tribal people. A tribe is a collection of kin groups acknowledging a common ancestry. The tribe may come together for joint action only on rare occasions. In daily life the most effective level of tribal organization was the clan, a subset of families sharing closer genealogical ties. Clans vied with each other for prestige and dominance, with blood feuds a common outcome. It was to their clan that people turned for support and protection.

Arabia is often imagined as a vast trackless waste. In reality it was a land of recognized boundaries, constituting the territory of its various tribal peoples including their jealously guarded rights to water and grazing. Defending the tribe's traditional rights was vital to survival and found expression through a code of tribal loyalty and honour with a heavy stress on martial values and military skills. The heroic deeds of famous warriors would be retold for generations in folk tales and epic odes.

The fierce independence fostered by nomadic life was noted by the Assyrian ruler Sargon II (721–705 BC), who wrote of 'the Arabs who live far away in the desert and who know neither overseers nor officials'.[14] While the difficulties of its environment kept central Arabia free from foreign conquest, this was not the case in the coastal regions. Yemen in the south and the eastern coasts on the Persian Gulf were at various times subject to foreign rule.

During the sixth century Arabia was squeezed between the two superpowers of the time: the contending empires of Christian Byzantium to the north and the Sassanid Empire of Persia to the east. A third influence was the Christian Abyssinian empire, which occupied Yemen and launched an unsuccessful assault on Mecca in the year Muhammad was born. These empires had clients and allies among the Arab tribes on their frontiers. Refugee rebels and heretics from within the Byzantine and Persian empires settled in Arabia. Various Christian communities are known to have existed, as did many Jewish tribes. It is clear that in diverse ways the Arabs were familiar and in contact with civilizations beyond their borders.

Muslim scholars and historians refer to the period before Muhammad's mission as the 'Age of Ignorance'. Their presentation implies that there was nothing but chaos: no government or rule of law, only perpetual warfare. Lawlessness certainly accompanies feuds and the frequency of looting and plundering. Yet, while tribal society lacks formal institutions it does have customary law and practices, even if their harsh conventions affronted the ethics of later commentators. The charge of 'ignorance', however, principally concerns pagan idol worship, which was the norm among pre-Islamic Arabs. Their various cults shared common features with the pagan religious beliefs of the ancient Middle East. Each tribe venerated its own guardian idol: the tribe of Kalb worshipped Wadd, a god shaped like a man; the tribe of Huzail worshipped Suwa, who was like a woman; the tribe of Bani Thaqif worshipped al-Lat, the mother goddess;

and Bani Kanana worshipped al-Uzza, the she devil, the goddess of love, sex and beauty. The main idol, worshipped by the Quraysh of Mecca, was Hubal, the shepherd. The stars, sun and moon were also worshipped – the morning star was called Athtar, the god Naakruh was Saturn or Mars, and Manat, a goddess of fate, represented the darkened moon. The main theme of their moral code was *muruwwa*, 'virility', which had no religious character but sustained the ethics of the noble warrior.

Gender relations

Pre-Islamic Arabs, despite contrary perceptions, were highly romantic. Both men and women boasted about their mastery of the art of love making. It was common for men to have scores of wives and partners, but women had customary rights and some independence, including possession of their own property and giving their consent to marriage. With multiple marriages and frequent divorce, a woman could reserve the right to divorce a husband who did not please her, and widowed or divorced women could remarry.

Pagan Arabia was a predominantly oral society, which does not mean that it was ignorant.

The Arabs were passionate about arts and letters, and cultivated poetry, oratory, discourses and folk tales.

In an oral society memory was much valued and history, customs and traditions were preserved through poetry, genealogical odes and stories. Children were taught their genealogy by heart going back 10 or even 20 generations, which is included in their own names: so-and-so, who is son (ibn, or bin) or son-of-so-and-so, who is son of . . . Everyone could recite classical poems by heart. The ritual year that brought together tribes from across Arabia included poetry recitals and competitions. In general, the pagan Arabs were renowned for their frankness, bravery, hospitality, generosity and love of independence, with a strong sense of their own dignity. United by a common language, set of beliefs and shared rituals, the Arabs had developed a sense of common identity by the sixth century.

▶ Mecca

Central Arabia had three cities of particular importance: Yathrib (which would later be renamed Medina), Taif and Mecca. Together they defined an area where commerce, art, culture and religious activities were concentrated. Yathrib, the most northerly, was an oasis with plentiful water that supported agriculture. It had a significant Jewish population working as jewellers, artisans and money lenders, among whom were many scholars familiar with the Hebrew Bible and the Talmud. Taif was an even more fertile oasis producing wheat, vines and fruit. By contrast, Mecca, barely a hundred kilometres north of Taif, was located in an arid valley dependent on trade for basic necessities. Mecca's source of fame and income was the pilgrims who came to visit the Kaaba – a cubed structure in the centre of the town. The Kaaba contained the idols worshipped by tribes from across Arabia, who came every year to pay homage to their gods.

Muslim accounts trace the origins of the Kaaba to Prophet Abraham. He came to this barren valley with his concubine Hagar and their infant son, Ismail, where he left them. When their meagre provisions were exhausted, Hagar searched desperately for water. In despair, she ran between the hills of Safa and Mawah, while the infant Ismail lay on the ground, crying with thirst. Then, God revealed a spring – Zamzam – to Hagar, and mother and child drank the water and settled in the area, which became a place for travellers to stop and rest. Later, when Abraham returned, and Ismail had grown up, God instructed the prophet to build a house as a symbol of his fidelity to monotheism. Together father and son built the Kaaba. Over time, the descendants of Ismail were banished from the city and the true significance of the Kaaba was lost. It became a pantheon full of statues for idol worship. The Islamic account of Abraham is one of many instances that differ from the biblical narratives. Such differences occasion much debate; however, the key point here is to appreciate the important role that the story of Abraham serves within Islam.

Mecca was a city state, with a governing council of 10 hereditary chiefs and a clear division of powers. There were ministers in charge of military affairs, foreign relations, municipal affairs and the all-important responsibility of guarding the Kaaba. Other ministers were responsible for looking after visiting pilgrims, providing them with provisions, escorting foreign dignitaries and overseeing ritual ceremonies and poetry recitals. And there were noted caravan leaders who supervised the caravan trade.

The city had another advantage. It was located on two major trading routes. One went south to Yemen and north to Syria and the Mediterranean; the other went east to Iraq and Iran and west to Abyssinia, Eastern Africa and the Red Sea ports of Egypt. The caravans converging on the city from the four directions were a major part of Mecca's economy. The Meccans had agreements with neighbouring empires – Iran, Byzantium and Abyssinia – that regulated trade into their territory, as well as with the tribes along the routes travelled by the caravans. Local tribes brought leather, livestock and the metal they mined from the mountains to Mecca. The frankincense, myrrh and balsam produced in Yemen were valuable trade goods central to religious ritual, medicinal and hygiene practices throughout the Middle East. Caravans carrying goods from Africa and the Far East, including spices, cloth, medicine and slaves, passed through Mecca. These caravans were like small cities on the move. They brought money, weapons, cereals, wine and slaves to the city. These the Meccans distributed throughout Arabia.

The significance of Mecca as an important trading city has been disputed.[15]

It has been suggested, for example, that the importance of Mecca was exaggerated by Muslim historians to give it a more momentous place in Islamic history.

It is claimed that the city was not on the international trade routes. Moreover, there is no archaeological evidence to suggest that it was a great centre of paganism.

Part of the problem is the lack of direct archaeological evidence in support of the classical Muslim historians. No excavations have been allowed in Mecca and Medina, regarded as sacred cities. Indeed modern redevelopment of Mecca has eradicated any such possibility. Where excavations have been undertaken they have found ample evidence of trade routes in the region. Recent significant finds have been made at Jurash in the Asir region of southwest Saudi Arabia, overlooking the Red Sea. Located in highlands 4,000 feet above sea level, Jurash was on an especially attractive route for caravans that transported incense, rare spices and other goods. They passed through the city to avoid the hot desert to the east. It would be natural for such caravans to pass through Mecca. There is also a treasure trove of ancient stone inscriptions, statues of gods and other material that provides evidence of Mecca as an important pagan centre.

Mecca was known to the ancient Greeks as a significant pagan city. It is, for example, mentioned in *Bibliotheca Historica* by Diodorus Siculus, the Greek historian who lived during the first century BC: 'a temple has been set-up there, which is very holy and exceedingly revered by all Arabians'.[16] It is also mentioned in the *Geography* of Claudius Ptolemy,[17] the Egyptian Roman citizen who lived around AD 90–168. It could hardly have been mentioned by these writers if it was a totally insignificant place where nothing ever happened.

Genealogical information, which the tribes took such pride in preserving, enabled Muslim historians such as ibn Ishaq, Tabari, ibn Sa'd and ibn Kathir (1301–73) to provide a picture of the ancient history of Mecca, complete with details of the tribal rulers of the city and their struggles for power. We know from these accounts that Mecca was ruled by a people of Arab stock known as Amalik (Amalekites of the Bible). The Amalik were replaced by the tribes of the Jurhum and Qatura, both originally from Yemen. Jurham were the first to settle in Mecca and became its dominant tribe and the sole religious and civil authority. The Jurham era lasted from around AD 200 to 400. There was a constant movement of tribes, with Yemeni tribes from southern Arabia migrating north. Mecca became a site of numerous political battles. The Jurham were ousted by one such tribe – the Khuza. It was during the Khuza period that pagan cults proliferated and were transformed into an economic institution, bringing pilgrims and wealth to Mecca.

The Khuza permitted the descendants of Ismail, the Quraysh, to return to the city, after seven centuries in exile.

Henceforth, the city's history is dominated by Qusayy, the leader of the Quraysh, and the sons and nephews who succeeded him. Drawing their information largely from material preserved in praise poems, it is certainly possible that Muslim historians may have exaggerated, for example in their descriptions of the excesses of the Jurham, the valour of Quassy or the nobility of the Quraysh. But the basic outline of this history cannot be denied and is accepted by the consensus of modern scholars.

Qusayy

Mecca was first built as a proper town by Zayd bin Kilab, popularly known as Qusayy, 'the little stranger', because he was born outside Mecca. He assembled his tribe, the Quraysh, and persuaded them to build their houses and live within the sacred area. Qusayy, who is Muhammad's fifth forefather, is believed to have died in AD 490.

It was against this historical and religious background that Muhammad emerged as a prophet.

3

Life before prophethood

Muhammad was born in Mecca in AD 570. His father, Abdullah, had died before his birth, and he was initially looked after by his grandfather, Abdul Muttalib. He was the chief of the Quraysh, the tribe into which Muhammad was born. According to the custom of the time, Muhammad was entrusted to a Bedouin foster mother, Halima, with whom he spent five years in the desert. A year after he was returned to his family, his mother, Amina, also died. Two years later, Abdul Muttalib, who was in his eighties, died too. Muhammad was now an orphan.

He came under the care of his uncle Abu Talib, a generous but poor man who could hardly provide for his own family. Muhammad had to earn his own livelihood and worked as shepherd looking after the herds of his family and neighbours. He was an intelligent boy, with, as was customary amongst the Arabs, an excellent memory and a keen sense of observation. He is said to have been quite mature for his tender years. At the age of 12, he accompanied his uncle on a business trip to Syria. It was a gruelling journey, but also an important source of education. He passed through Madyan, Wadi ul-Qura and the territory of the Thamud, and his attentive ears listened to the conversations of the people he met about these cities and their histories. He also witnessed the fruit gardens of Syria – a sharp contrast to the barren hills of Mecca. And he met Christian monks, heard them speak about their scriptures and came to know of the Byzantine Empire.

The journey to Syria awakened his interest in travel. He frequently accompanied his relatives to the neighbouring markets of Ukaz, Majannah and Dhu al Majaz, where he listened to the speeches of Christians and Jews who condemned the paganism of the people of Arabia. And he attended poetry recitals and heard of his ancestors, their conquests and chivalry, the genealogy of his tribe and the inhabitants of Mecca, and came to appreciate the power and eloquence of Arabic poetry. By the time he was 20, he joined merchant caravans, as an agent of rich Meccans, and travelled frequently on business. During these journeys and commercial transactions, he acquired the nickname of Al-Amin, the trustworthy one. He also became known for his qualities of patience, diligence, moderation and fortitude.

Name

Muhammad is the most common name in the world.

Nickname

Muhammad's nickname before he became a prophet was Al-Amin, the most trustworthy.

War of Fijar

When Muhammad was about 15, a feud broke out between Arab tribes over the ransacking of a caravan. It escalated to what is known as the War of Fijar, or the unholy war, because it took place in a month considered sacred by the Meccans. Muhammad participated in the war. His task was to pick up the stray arrows thrown by the enemy and hand them back to his uncle, Abu Talib, the chief of his tribe in the war.

This picture of the early life of Muhammad is largely based on literary documents that were complied one of two centuries after his death. Many of the stories included in these accounts are historically questionable, some are simply legends created by later generations of Muslims to provide a sanctimonious aura around Muhammad's personality. During his travels to Syria, for example, Muhammad is said to have come across a Christian monk called Bahira in Busra. He invited members of Muhammad's party for dinner. They left young Muhammad behind to look after the baggage. Bahira specifically asked that Muhammad join him for dinner. When Muhammad appeared before him, Bahira examined Muhammad for signs of prophethood and subjected him to a series of questions. When he finished, he told Abu Talib to guard Muhammad carefully, especially against the Jews who saw him as a threat, and a great future awaited his nephew.

Another story tells us that Muhammad was visited by 'two white-clad' angels when he was still an infant in the care of Halima. The angels grabbed him and 'laid him on the ground; then they opened up his chest and lunged their hands in it'.[18] Apparently, the angels took out a black clot, the centre of evil, and threw it away to purify him, and later washed his heart and chest with snow. The function of the story is to demonstrate that Muhammad was protected from the temptation of evil from his infant days. He is also said to have participated in an alliance, known as the Pact of the Virtuous, which was established to uphold the principle of justice and support the oppressed. As a young man, Muhammad had many inspirational dreams and was interested only in the contemplation of his soul.

Such stories are a later attempt to rationalize Muhammad's special spiritual position and to infuse his personality with divine character. But we can be certain that the honesty and integrity of Muhammad the man, as well as his success as a merchant, brought him to the attention of the rich widow, Khadija. She had been married twice, and her second husband had left her considerable property. She needed a mercantile agent and engaged Muhammad's services. He went on a business trip to Syria on her behalf, accompanied by one of her servants, and returned with considerable success. The servant dutifully gave a full report of the journey to Khadija, describing Muhammad's honesty in dealing with her affairs, his loyalty to her and his gentle treatment of her. All this confirmed what she had already learned of Muhammad's character and she proposed marriage. Muhammad accepted and they were married almost immediately. She was 40; he was 25.

Muhammad had six children with Khadijah: two sons and four daughters. The sons died in infancy. Muhammad's desire for a son was fulfilled in Zaid ibn Harithah, presented to him as a slave whom he freed and adopted. The daughters – Zaynab, Ruqayyah, Um Kulthum and Fatimah – grew up and were married. After the advent of Islam, Zaynab (d. 630) separated from her husband and Ruqayyah and Um Kulthum were divorced by their husbands. Ruqayyah then married Uthman but died in

624 when Uthman married Um Kulthum (d. 631). Fatimah, married to her cousin Ali, alone survived Muhammad – dying a few months after him in 632.

By all accounts, husband and wife were very happy together, although they naturally mourned the loss of their sons. Muhammad's life during this period was comfortable and secure. He had ample time to think and reflect. Given his insight, he was clearly perturbed by the injustice, social upheaval and idol worship he saw around him. It was customary among thoughtful and pious Arabs to go on an annual retreat and devote some time to prayer and inner reflection. The practice was called *tahannuth* and it involved seeking an empty place far from the crowds to sit quietly and think. It was in this practice that Muhammad found the best means to satisfy his inner thirst. He found an apt place: a cave called Hira, some three kilometres north of Mecca. There he would sit for hours contemplating and meditating.

▶ Hanifs and rebuilding the Kaaba

A man sitting in a cave contemplating the cosmos is not necessarily a tabula rasa.

Muslims like to see the prophet as a clean sheet of paper have written on the words of God. He is said to have been illiterate, he could neither read nor write – but hardly anyone in his society could. That, however, does not mean that he was uneducated. He had acquired considerable knowledge through his travels, accumulated information through the processes of oral transmission, gained considerable experience and skills in the marketplace, knew his tribal history and gained understanding of ruined civilizations, even though he was not formally instructed. He certainly knew how to think, plan, distinguish between fact and fable and critically sift information. While he was not capable of reading the scriptures of Jews and Christians, it is likely that he possessed some literate skills. And he had already found God even before he went to Cave Hira.

Mecca had a group of people who emphasized the faith of Abraham, and kept themselves away from the idol worshippers. Some of these monotheists were undoubtedly Christians and Jews, but some did not subscribe to any specific religion. Muhammad belonged to this group of monotheists, who were known as *Hanifs*.[19] The Hanifs retained the tenets of the religion of Abraham and believed that submission was due only to One God, and they practised tahannuth (embarking on retreats for reflection and meditation). They also believed that the Kaaba was the house dedicated to One God by its builder Abraham. The Hanifs often rebuked the Meccans for their pagan ways, and suffered the consequences. One of them, Zaid bin Amr, who rejected not just Christianity and Judaism but also Islam, was a friend of Muhammad and may have been his early mentor. His monotheistic views led to discord with the

Quraysh, who drove him out of Mecca to live in Syria and Iraq. Another member of the group, Ubayd Allah ibn Jahsh, embraced Islam but later changed his mind, then embraced Christianity and died a Christian. His wife, Umm Habibah, remained a Muslim and later married Muhammad and became a 'Mother of the Faithful'. Some Hanifs also came into conflict with Muhammad later in his life.

While Muhammad frequently went on his retreats, he did not withdraw altogether from the public life of Mecca. When Muhammad was 36, around the year AD 605, the draperies on the outer wall of the Kaaba accidently caught fire. The building was affected and could not bear the brunt of the torrential rains that followed. The Kaaba had no ceiling and its treasures were exposed. The Meccans feared that they would be robbed. It had to be rebuilt, but the Meccans feared that rebuilding the Kaaba with doors and a ceiling might unleash a curse upon them. While they were contemplating what to do, there was a shipwreck in the nearby port of Jeddah. The ship belonged to a Byzantine trader, who was a carpenter, and the salvage provided valuable wood that could be used for rebuilding the Kaaba. Reluctantly, the work to reconstruct the Kaaba was undertaken.

All the citizens of the city participated in the reconstruction, and all contributed according to their means. Muhammad was there too; his shoulders were injured from carrying the stones from the nearby mountains to the Kaaba. When the building was ready, it was time to put the Black Stone in its place. The Black Stone in the wall of the Kaaba probably dates back to the time of Abraham himself. Its main function is to identify the place where

▲ The Kaaba

the ritual of circumambulation – going around the Kaaba a number of times – begins. All the tribes of Mecca wanted the honour of transporting the stone to its place. There was a real danger of bloodshed as nobles of the Mecca jostled and swore that no one would rob them of this honour. Eventually it was decided that matters should be left to providence. The gathering of nobles around the Kaaba agreed that the arbitration of the first person to walk through one of the gates of the enclosure would be accepted. The first one to pass through the gate was Muhammad, who had turned up for work as usual. Given that he was popularly known as 'the most trustworthy' (Al-Amin), the gathering accepted his adjudication without hesitation. Muhammad placed a sheet of cloth on the ground, put the stone on it, and asked the chiefs of all the city's tribes to lift the cloth together. Then he alone placed the stone on its proper place. Everyone was satisfied.

It was after the rebuilding of the Kaaba that Muhammad became more and more absorbed with his spiritual quest. His visits to Cave Hira became more frequent. There he would pray night and day, and fasted for long periods. On occasions, he would come down from the cave for a stroll and then return to the cave – always pondering, questioning, reconsidering.

Highly disciplined in his spiritual practices and steadfast in his search for truth, he could not tear himself away from his solitude.

This went on for over six months. Whenever he returned from the cave, his troubled inner thoughts could be read on his face, leading Khadija to ask if he was feeling unwell.

By now he was 40; he had been going on retreats for five years. Up to now he had led a quiet life following its natural course in relatively peaceful obscurity. His spiritual discipline enabled him to catch a glimpse of the truth, to realize that beyond material existence life had a more important spiritual dimension. Then something totally unexpected happened.

4

The prophet
in Mecca

One night, according to Muslim tradition, Muhammad was meditating inside Cave Hira and had fallen asleep. Suddenly, he awoke in abject terror, his whole body trembling. Later, Muhammad himself described the sensation as if an angel had gripped him in a tight embrace that threatened to squeeze the breath and life out of him. As he lay there, shattered, he heard a voice.

> *The voice commanded him: 'Read!'*
> *'I can't read, I'm not of those who read,' Muhammad replied.*
> *The voice repeated the command: 'Read.'*
> *He replied again: 'I'm not of those who read.'*
> *'Read,' he was ordered again.*
> *'What shall I read?' he asked in a trembling voice.*
> *The voice responded with what is considered the first revelation of what became the Qur'an:*
> *'Read,' said the voice, 'in the name of your Lord who created:*
> *He created man from a clot.*
> *Read! Your Lord is most Bountiful,*
> *Who taught by the pen,*
> *Taught man what he knew not.'*
>
> (96: 1–5)

Revelation is a complex, mysterious phenomenon, not easy to either explain or comprehend. In common with other prophets, Muhammad found the experience a physical trial. Isaiah, for example, had his lips burnt with a coal before he could speak. Jeremiah said, 'My Lord God, I'm a child, I can't speak. I don't know how to speak.' And Muhammad said, 'I am not of those who read.'

But was it a revelatory experience? Clearly this is the crux of belief for Muslims. For those who do not believe, there are no independent means of verification, no actual objective tests that can be applied. Western scholars have offered a number of explanations. Muhammad was a rather good poet and revelation is the product of his imagination, rather like William Blake's prophetic poetry. Or Muhammad could be an epileptic and the revelation a product of epileptic seizures. Or he could have been helped by Jews and Christians to compose the revelation. Such explanations hardly rise to the level of convincing argument for something as momentous as asserting that one has heard the word of God from an angel. Ultimately a matter of belief is just that, and a matter on which casting around for supposedly rational explanations adds nothing to our understanding. The Muslim position is that Muhammad saw the revelation in his mind and in his heart, which enabled him to retain and recite something profound and eternal. The evidence for his revelation is the Qur'an itself. Those moved by its power will believe; others will seek alternative explanations.

Initially, Muhammad himself was unsure about what had happened. He was fearful, full of doubt and thought he was possessed. He left the cave, pale and trembling, climbed down the mountain, and ran straight to his beloved wife, Khadija. She had no doubts about her husband's experience. At this juncture, we come across another one of the many apocryphal stories that abound in Muslim tradition. Khadijah is said to have taken Muhammad to her cousin, Waraqa ibn Nawfal, one of the

Hanifs who was specially versed in Christian tradition, who confirmed that Muhammad was indeed a recipient of revelation.

Muhammad's own doubts were not lessened. After his initial experience in the cave during the month of Ramadan in the year AD 610, there was silence for the next two years. He became desperate, and even began to think that he was deluded. Or perhaps, he thought, he was lacking in the qualities that God required. But his doubts were similar to those of other prophets: Moses, who doubted his own abilities and qualifications to be a prophet; Jesus, who faced a similar crisis in his life; and Buddah, who was constantly plagued by doubts.

▲ 'Muhammad' in Arabic, written as a mirror image of itself

Then the doubts evaporated. One morning, while Muhammad sat in Cave Hira thinking that he had been abandoned, he experienced another revelation:

> Consider, the bright morning hours
> And the night when it grows still and dark
> Your Lord has not forsaken you
> Nor does he hate you
> And the future will be better than the past
> Your Lord is sure to give you so much that you will be satisfied.
> Did He not find you an orphan and shelter you?
> Did He not find you lost and guide you?
> Did He not find you in need and make you self-sufficient?
>
> (93: 1–8)

More revelations followed at intervals and continued until shortly before Muhammad's death in 632. They always came in short bursts and they always terrified him. He felt as though his soul had been torn away from him. Sometimes he found the verbal content to be quite clear, but at other times it was more allegorical and metaphorical.

▶ The Qur'an and Islam

The revelations – the Qur'an, literally 'the recitation' – urged Muhammad to preach. He started, in secret, among his own family circle. His wife Khadija was the first convert. She was followed by his teenage cousin and ward, Ali, and his adopted son, Zaid. Also amongst the early converts was Abu Bakr, a successful businessman and a long-standing friend. Other converts were mainly young and the dispossessed. Many came from what we would today call the working classes, both men and women. Some were slaves, among them an Abyssinian called Bilal, who would become famous as the first person to publicly call the faithful to prayer. But not everyone in his family was open to Muhammad's message. The prophet failed to convince his uncle Abu Talib, who had brought him up as his own son.

Muhammad's main message was simple and direct. It was, in the words of the Qur'an, 'Say, "He is God the One, God the eternal. He begot no one, nor is He begotten. No one is comparable to Him" ' (112: 1–4). To the people of seventh-century Mecca, it was a radical message. It undermined everything that the pagan Arabs believed. Fervently attached to their gods, they saw Muhammad's unequivocal monotheism as a direct challenge, an act of subversion. Not surprisingly, they were hostile to his message.

The message also sought to reform the customs of the people of Mecca. Muhammad wanted an end to infanticide, tribal warfare and murder, which he found loathsome. His preaching included a list of forbidden acts, loosely analogous as his 'Ten Commandments':

> Say, 'Come I will tell you what your Lord has really forbidden you.
>
> 1. Do not ascribe anything as a partner to Him;
> 2. Be good to your parents;

3. Do not kill your children for fear of poverty; We shall provide for you and for them;
4. Do not indulge in shameful acts, whether openly or in secret;
5. Do not take life that God has made sacred, except through (due process of) law;
    This is what He commands you to do; perhaps you will use your reason.
6. Stay well away from the property of orphans, except with the best of intentions, until they come of age;
7. Give full measure and weight, according to justice;
8. Whenever you speak, be just even if it concerns a relative;
9. Keep any promises you make in God's name;
    This is what He commands you to do, so you may take heed –
10. This is my path, leading straight, so follow it and do not follow other ways.

(6: 151–3)

What Muhammad preached came to be known as Islam, meaning 'peace' and 'surrender'. It was an egalitarian message, aimed at liberating people from pagan beliefs, emphasizing compassion and the rule of law.

Muhammad's main concern was building a loving, just and equitable society. It is wrong to stockpile wealth, to build a personal fortune, but good to give alms and distribute the wealth of society, he told his followers. We are all brothers who should help each other, help the poor and the needy, cooperate with one another in doing good and virtuous deeds, and shun vice and aggression, he declared. Be tolerant and moderate in speech and action, generous and forgiving, and avoid conceit and vanity, extravagance and hypocrisy, he announced.

After three years of preaching privately among friends, Muhammad was commanded, in 615, to 'proclaim openly what you have been commanded to say, and ignore the idolaters' (15: 94).

He invited 40 of the leading citizens to dinner. His criticism of the greed and avarice of the city's businessmen infuriated the rich Meccans. They were incensed by his attacks on their customs and traditions. The leaders of the ruling tribes were disturbed by the idea of people abandoning the gods of their ancestors, the very gods who justified their status and power and who, by attracting pilgrims to the city, brought in the wealth that underpinned the hierarchy of Meccan society. The rulers of Mecca, the Quraysh, felt that their power and influence were threatened. Something had to be done.

A group of leaders and elders from the Quraysh went to see Muhammad's uncle, Abu Talib. How could he, one of the most revered men of the tribe, they asked, allow his nephew to abuse our gods and question the ancient customs and traditions that were the basis of their way of life? You must stop him, they insisted. Abu Talib summoned his nephew. 'How could you put such a strain on me and our clan?', he demanded to know. 'Have you forgotten that I looked after you from the age of eight? Spare me and spare yourself,' Abu Talib pleaded. With tears in his eyes, Muhammad replied: 'By God if they put the sun in my right hand and the moon on my left on condition that I abandon this course, I would not abandon it until God has made me victorious or I perish.'[20]

Abu Talib admired his nephew's determination; he pledged to continue to protect Muhammad and his religion – a religion he did not believe in. The Meccans now changed their tactics. Would Muhammad accept wealth and riches to stop his hatred of their idols? How about the leadership of Mecca? When all the proposals were rejected, the Meccans started to insult and harass Muhammad at every opportunity. Dirt was thrown at him, thorns were laid in his path. He was stoned.

Muhammad had the protection of Abu Talib and his clan. Most of his followers had no clan protection and became victims of extreme violence. Some were thrown on burning coals, a newly converted woman was stabbed to death and others were cruelly beaten and tortured. Bilal, the African slave of a Meccan businessman, was dragged through the desert by a horse for days on end.

▶ Jafar's testimony

Muhammad became concerned for the welfare of his followers. He decided to spare them further suffering and find a safe haven for them. Nowhere in Arabia seemed sufficiently safe from the power of the Meccan elite. His family had trade relations with Abyssinia, the Axumite kingdom ruled by a Christian monarch. He advised some of his followers to migrate to Abyssinia. In 615, a initial group of refugees secretly left Mecca. In all, 83 Muslims with their families eventually made the trip to Abyssinia. They included Muhammad's daughter Ruquayyah, her husband Uthman and Jafar, the son of Muhammad's uncle Abu Talib.

The Meccans were incensed by this exodus. They hastily sent a delegation to the Negus, the king of Abyssinia, to persuade him to force the refugees to return to Mecca. The Negus wanted to hear what the refugees had to say for themselves. 'What is this religion that has caused you to separate from your people?', he asked. The reply, on behalf of the refugees, was given by Jafar. It provides a good indication of why, against all the opposition, people in Mecca were converting to Islam.

'O king,' said Jafar, 'we were in a state of ignorance and immorality, worshipping idols, eating carrion, committing all sorts of injustices. We honoured no relative and assisted no neighbour. The strong amongst us exploited the weak. Then God sent us a Prophet, one of our own people, whose lineage, truthfulness, loyalty and purity was well known to us. He called us to worship God alone. He commanded us always to tell the truth, to fulfil our trust and promise, to assist relatives, to be good to neighbours, to abstain from bloodshed, to avoid fornication, perjury and false witness. He commanded us not to rob the wealth of orphans or falsely accuse married women. We believed in him and followed him. But our people tried to sway us away, persecuted us and inflicted upon us great suffering to persuade us to return to the old way. As our life became intolerable in Mecca, we chose you and your country and came here to live under your protection in justice and peace.'[21]

The Negus asked to hear something of Muhammad's message. Jafar is said to have recited a portion of Chapter 19 of the Qur'an, surah Maryam, verses 17–26, which concern the assumption of Mary the mother of Jesus. Nothing was more likely to appeal to this Christian court. When Jafar had finished, the Negus and his bishops were in tears. There was no doubt that the refugees would be safe in Abyssinia.

In Mecca, opposition to Muhammad became even more draconian. A boycott was imposed on Muhammad's entire clan. No one was to have any dealings with them. They were not allowed to intermarry, trade or even buy food from the markets of Mecca. Abu Talib thought it wise to withdraw his clan to a valley outside Mecca for safety. There they had limited food and provision and soon their supplies ran out. Famished, some had to eat leaves to survive. But they bore the hardship with forbearance and fortitude.

The Quraysh were convinced that it was only a matter of time before Abu Talib's clan would perish, or Muhammad would abandon his mission. However, the conscience of some inhabitants of Mecca was stirred by the plight of their neighbours. They objected to the boycott. Eventually it was abandoned and Muhammad and his companions were allowed to return to the city.

The abuser who is ill

A Jewish woman regularly used to insult Muhammad and throw rubbish at him whenever he passed below her house. One day, she failed to abuse him or throw rubbish at him. Intrigued, he enquired about her and discovered that she was ill. He immediately visited her and wished her a speedy recovery.

The experience had taken its toll and Muhammad was about to face more anguish. Abu Talib, his uncle and protector, fell ill during 619. Muhammad tried to convince the dying Abu Talib to accept Islam. Abu Talib declined, saying such a conversion would convince no one and would be done only to please his nephew. Feeling despondent, Muhammad began to cry. At that moment, he received a revelation: 'You Prophet cannot guide everyone you love to truth; it is God who guides whosoever He wills. He knows best those who will follow guidance' (28: 56). It was an important lesson. Faith, the revelation had declared, is personal, and conviction comes from both the heart and the mind. Islam was not to be forced upon anyone and faith had to be willingly embraced: 'Let there be no compulsion in religion', the Quran asserted (2: 256). A few months later, Khadija, his beloved wife, friend and councillor, who had supported him for 25 years, also died. It must have seemed that his whole world was collapsing.

The Satanic Verses

The incident of the Satanic Verses, made famous by Salman Rushdie's novel of the same title, is supposed to have occurred in 615. It is reported that during the darkest period of his time in Mecca, Muhammad acknowledged pagan beliefs. The Quranic verse, '[disbelievers] consider al-Lat and al-Uzza and the third one, al-Manat' (53: 19–20) was supposedly followed by 'these are the high flying cranes, whose intercession is to be sought'. The Quraysh, overjoyed, declared that 'Muhammad had spoken of our gods in splendid fashion'. Then the archangel Gabriel came to the prophet and said, 'What have you done Muhammad? You have read to these people something I did not bring from God and you have said what He did not say to you.' Muhammad was struck with grief. The verses were annulled and replaced with 'they are nothing but names you have invented yourselves, you and your forefathers' (53: 23). The story is described in ibn Ishaq's *Life of Muhammad* but most Muslim scholars regard it as total fiction. Ibn Ishaq himself declared it a fabrication by the pagans. It also goes against everything Muhammad believed and stood for.

In a society where lack of clan protection was tantamount to a death sentence, the death of Abu Talib left Muhammad vulnerable and exposed. The leadership of his clan fell into the hands of his most virulent opponents. Attacks against him increased; there was even an attempt to strangle him to death. He decided to seek refuge in the nearby town of Taif, hoping it would be more hospitable. But the people of Taif were as wedded to their ancient gods as the citizens of Mecca. The shrine of the goddess al-Lat was the centre of life there. And the followers of al-Lat did not take kindly to Muhammad's message of one, omnipotent, god. He was attacked, beaten and thrown out of town. In traditional accounts, this period is usually referred to as 'the year of sorrow'.

▶ The Night Journey

On his return to Mecca, under the cover of darkness, Muhammad decided to spend the night in the house of his cousin, Hind, the daughter of Abu Talib. Grief stricken and in need of solace, he withdrew to his inner self. Just before dawn, he had a profound spiritual experience. Known as 'the Night Journey', it was a mystical vision of a journey (called *Isra*) that took him to Jerusalem from where he ascended to the heavens and was greeted by previous Prophets – Adam, Abraham, Moses and Jesus – before rising further (called the *Miraj*) to God's Presence. The Qur'an described the event in these words: 'Glory to Him who made His servant travel by night from the sacred place of worship to the furthest place of worship, whose surroundings we have blessed, to show him some of Our signs' (17: 1).

The Night Journey is one of the most important events in Muhammad's life. It is central to the theology of Islam, and has inspired generations of Muslim mystics, known as Sufis, to seek a similar experience of the divine.

▲ Mecca as depicted on a seventeenth-century Turkish tile

Muslims derive their understanding of paradise from this vision, and it led to the establishment of five daily prayers and made Jerusalem significant as the third holiest city of Islam. The Dome of the Rock on the Temple Mount in Jerusalem was built over the place where Muhammad is said to have begun his ascent to heaven.

Like all mystical experiences, we have no way of validating the event. Sayings of Muhammad relating to it are disputed within Muslim tradition; even the date of the Night Journey is uncertain. All we can say is that it took place between 620 and 622. Details of the journey have been embellished and have also become the subject of resplendent artworks. It has been subject to a number of different interpretations. Some Muslims see the journey in physical terms: Muhammad literally travelled, in the proverbial blink of an eye, from Mecca to Jerusalem, and then ascended to Heaven. Some stories suggest that he sat on the back of a celestial guide, a winged beast that was part horse and part mule, called *Buraq*, or Lightning, and travelled above familiar caravan trails that are identified along the route.

For others, the Isra and Miraj are purely mystical experiences. The Qur'an describes the Night Journey as a vision, and in allegorical, metaphysical terms:

> *Someone firm in strength, who stood on the highest horizon and then approached – coming down until he was two bow-lengths away or even closer – and revealed to God's servant what He revealed . . . A second time he saw him: by the lote tree beyond which none may pass near the Garden of Restfulness, when the tree was covered in nameless splendour. His sight never wavered, nor was it too bold, and he saw some of the greatest signs of his Lord.*
>
> *(53: 9–10, 13–18)*

Both Hind and Muhammad's young wife Aisha are recorded in the traditional sources as asserting that the Night Journey was accomplished while the body of Muhammad did not stir and remained asleep in Mecca.

The transcendent vision contained in the Night Journey replaced despair with hope, goodness, truth and beauty. Muhammad was filled with a new vigour and became even more determined to spread his message.

Hijra: the migration

Despite all the opposition, and the plots against him, Muhammad continued to preach. He spent most of his time preaching outside the city, in the valleys and settlements surrounding Mecca. At a place called Aqaba, between Mount Hira and Mina a few miles from Mecca, he met and preached to a group of six men from the northern city of Yathrib who had come to attend the annual pilgrimage and fair that was part of the ritual year in Mecca. They listened earnestly to Muhammad's words. The meeting ended with their conversion and an accord. The men would take the message of Islam back to their city and return the following year. Muhammad sent some of his followers to Yathrib to read the Qur'an to them and instruct them in religion.

The next year a bigger delegation arrived, some 73 men and two women, to meet with Muhammad at Aqaba. This meeting led to the second covenant of Aqaba in which the visitors agreed to protect Muhammad as they would protect their own women and children. On this occasion, an entire tribe from Medina, Banu Abd Al-Ashhal, converted to Islam. They invited Muhammad to come and join them in Yathrib. This was a new kind of alliance: an accord based not on family, clan or tribal allegiances, as was the norm, but on faith.

It did not take the Quraysh long to discover that Muhammad had made an alliance with some tribes of Yathrib. They regarded it as an attempt to wage war against them. The tension between Muhammad and his enemies in Mecca reached boiling point. The Quraysh devoted considerable time to thinking how they could outmanoeuvre Muhammad and destroy his faith. Finally, they decided to kill the prophet. Their plan was both simple and ingenious: one member from every clan in Mecca would stab Muhammad at the same time, thus making it impossible for Muhammad's own clan to avenge his murder. On the appointed night the selected group surrounded Muhammad's house. They were assured of Muhammad's presence when they spotted a sleeping figure wrapped in his familiar green cloak. They did not enter in deference to Arab notions of chivalry because they were aware that there were women in the house.

At dawn, with daggers drawn, the assassins rushed into Muhammad's house. But instead of finding the Prophet, they found his young cousin, Ali, sleeping in his bed. Muhammad, aware of the plot, had slipped out unnoticed during the night. He then met up with his friend and companion, Abu Bakr, and together they set off on the journey to Yathrib.

The young men of the Quraysh chosen to kill Muhammad were enraged. They organized an armed party and set out in pursuit to hunt him down. Muhammad and Abu Bakr had decided to hide in the cave of Thawr; it was to the south of Mecca, in exactly the opposite direction to the normal route. This was kept a well-guarded secret. Yet, the search party managed to trace their steps up to the foothills of Mount Thwar, from where the trail ran cold and the trackers were brought to a standstill. They searched for three days but could find no trace of Muhammad or his footprints. Eventually, they gave up and returned to Mecca.

When the coast was clear, Muhammad and Abu Bakr continued their journey to Yathrib. As they did not take the usual caravan route but kept to the desert their journey was exceptionally hard. There was nothing to alleviate the remorseless sun, nor was there water to quench their thirst. They travelled for seven days, hiding from the heat of the sun and potential threats during the day, and moving swiftly at night. Muhammad's followers, the entire Muslim community, had already slowly and systematically slipped out of Mecca and made the journey to Yathrib. Back in Mecca, Ali was returning the deposits and trusts that Meccans had kept with Muhammad and was repaying his loans or returning other things he had borrowed.

Muhammad received a rapturous reception in Medina. In his honour, the name of the city was later changed. Forever after Yathrib would be known as Medinat an-nabi, or 'the city of the Prophet', usually shortened simply to Medina.

Islamic calendar

The Prophet's migration from Mecca to Medina, known as the *hijra*, took place in AD 622. It marks the beginning of the Islamic calendar. It is a lunar calendar consisting of 12 lunar months, which are not synchronized with the seasons. It drifts by 10 or 11 days a year, and the seasonal relation repeats about every 33 lunar years. The dates are given as AH, anno hejirae or after hijra.

His life as a prophet in Mecca had been akin to being in a crucible: relentless persecution, constant threats to his life, continuous oppression of his followers, and full of personal loss and tragedies. Yet he endured all this with patience and good humour and was ever ready to forgive his tormentors. Even his sworn enemies had complete trust in him and respected his integrity, humility, kindness and compassion. Muhammad went out of his way to avoid direct confrontations with the Quraysh, and when faced with violence always chose a non-violent way out of his predicaments.

The Muslim community in Mecca was small, with fewer than a hundred people. Life had been hard and it was not possible to keep records. This is why the Meccan period of Muhammad's life is not as well documented as it should be. The revelations of this period, which constitute about two-thirds of the Qur'an, also have a distinctive character. They tend to be short, emphasize the spiritual aspects of life and dwell on the source and origins of Muhammad's mission. His mission, the revelations state, is only to teach the essence of faith. He is told that the message itself is not new, but a continuation of the message sent to all the previous prophets: 'We have sent revelation to you [Prophet] as We did to Noah and the prophets after him, to Abraham, Ishmael, Isaac, Jacob, and the Tribes, to Jesus, Job, Jonah, Aaron, and Solomon – to David We gave the book [of Psalms] – to other messengers We have already mentioned to you, and also to some We have not' (4: 163). The Meccan chapters contain no legislative commandments; they exhort, guide and advise.

The situation of Muslims changed significantly with their migration to Medina. In addition to the Muslims who came from Mecca, known as *Muhajirs* (immigrants or refugees), there were mass conversions amongst the *Ansars*, the helpers and supporters, the people of Medina who invited him to the city. The Muslim community was still relatively small (it doubled in size – some accounts say there were 150 Muhajirs and 50 Ansars) but Muhammad was largely among his followers and the Muslims had a sense of autonomy.

Muhammad could now devote some time to building a just and equitable community.

Thus, as the emphasis of his life changed so did the tone and character of the revelations, which now had legislative content, though the Qur'an has fewer prescriptive injunctions than one might expect. It describes itself as a book of guidance rather than a book of law.

The various nobles of Medina vied with each other to invite Muhammad to stay in their house, but he refused. It was a delicate matter of no small political import. Rather than opt for a particular location he decided to settle where his camel came to a halt. It was a piece of land belonging to two orphan brothers. He was offered the land as a gift but again declined and insisted that its owners should be paid adequately. He ordered that a mosque should be built on the land. The whole Muslim community, including Muhammad himself, joined in the building of the mosque. As they built the mosque, Muhammad sang:

> There's no life but the life of the next world
> O God, have mercy on the muhajirin and the ansar.

Ali, his cousin, joined in with his own poem:

> There's one that labours night and day
> To build us mosques of brick and clay
> And one who turns from dust away.[22]

The mosque came to be known as the Prophet's Mosque, and Muhammad also built a small house beside it. He declared that all Muslims were brothers and paired each Muhajir with an Ansar brother – an act that raised the prestige of the locals and ensured the material welfare of the immigrants. The Ansars invited the Muhajir into their houses and opened their purse-strings to them. Initially, the Muhajirs accepted the hospitality with joy, but they did not want to be a burden on their brothers in Medina. The traders among them quickly established themselves and were able to make a sustainable living. Those who could not engage in trade took to farming the land owned by the Ansars under a system of sharecropping. The arrangements not only provided for mutual assistance between the two groups, they also established the bonds of real fraternity. The Muslims were now forged into a strong, indivisible community.

During this initial period in Medina, Muhammad also established the call to prayer – the *Adhan,* which throughout

▲ Entrance to Cave Hira

the Muslim world summons the faithful to prayer five times a day. As Bilal, the slave who was tortured in Mecca, had the most beautiful voice, he was asked to make the first call to prayer. Other religious institutions, such as the obligatory poor tax, *zakat*, and fasting during the month of Ramadan, were also established.

'God is Great. God is Great. I witness that there is no god but God. I witness that Muhammad is the Prophet of God. Rise to prayer. Rise to felicity. God is Great. God is Great. There is no god but God.'

Muhammad asked his followers to show kindness and mercy to others, avoid pride and haughtiness, be just and modest in all matters, and pay attention to personal hygiene.

As for himself, he led a rather ascetic life, shunning all extravagance and luxuries.

In Mecca, the Quraysh were seething with anger. They had managed to throw Muhammad out of the city of his birth, where he grew up, met and married his beloved Khadija, and where he had his first experience of revelation. However, in Medina, Muhammad presented an even bigger threat to their power and privilege because he could now preach freely and spread his message more widely than ever before. The Meccans became more determined to crush Muhammad and exterminate the nascent Muslim community.

6

The Constitution
of Medina

Despite the conversion to Islam of many inhabitants of Medina after Muhammad's arrival, Muslims were still a minority in the city. A year after the hijra, the total Muslim population was no more than 1,500 people. Moreover, the immigrants from Mecca and their helpers, natives of Medina, were from different tribes and their different tribal customs led to some tension among the Muslims. The dominant group within the city, in numbers as well as political and military power, were the Jewish tribes. It was to be expected that they had some resentment about the new authority wielded by Muhammad. And there remained a sizeable number of pagans who had not accepted the message of Muhammad. Thus, Medina was a divided city. The two chief Arab factions and their Jewish allies were at war with each other. Indeed, this was one of the main reasons Muhammad had been invited to the city: to reconcile the murderous differences between the tribes of Medina. He saw his main task as forming a united community out of these heterogeneous elements.

Muhammad went out of his way to cultivate good relationships with the Jewish tribes. He visited their chiefs and nobles. He fasted with them. And, like them, he turned his face towards Jerusalem during prayer. Eventually, he persuaded the Jews, and some pagan tribes, to freely enter into an alliance of mutual cooperation with the Muslims.

The result was the formation of a new political community forged from the different groups in Medina – Muslims, Jews, Christians and pagans. With the consent of all groups, Muhammad endowed the city with a written constitution.

The 'Constitution of Medina' is the earliest and one of most important documents from the time of Muhammad.[23] A number of versions of this constitution have survived, along with some letters of Muhammad. Although commonly referred to as the 'Constitution of Medina', in the original Arabic it was called simply *Kitab*, or 'Book'.

The Constitution of Medina is not a constitution in the modern sense, more a social contract: an agreement between different groups to work and function as a unified community.

The document, dictated by Muhammad, defines the relationship between the members of three groups: the Muhajirun, or the immigrant Quraysh who came from Mecca; the Ansar, or the Helpers, the Medinans who converted to Islam; and the Jewish tribes of Medina. It provides an overall legal framework for the social and political conduct of the community. The Constitution of Medina uses the language and formulae of the customary law and legal practices of Medina on issues such as blood money or compensation to express the rights and responsibilities of the citizens. A unified document (some scholars, however, suggest it is a collection of documents), it consists of two clearly defined parts: the first refers to the Muhajirun and the Ansar, while the second addresses the Jews of Medina.

Constitution of Medina, Article 25

'The Jews of Banu Awf shall be considered as a community [*ummah*] along with the Believers, the Jews have their religion and the Muslims have their religion. This applies to their allies and the original members of the tribe. But whoever shall be guilty of oppression or violation [of treaty] shall put to trouble none but his own person and the members of his house.'

The Constitution begins with what looks like a declaration of independence. Its second clause states: 'they constitute one ummah to the exclusion of all other men.' 'They' refers to Muslims, Jews and other client tribes; together they assert the autonomy of their newly formed community. Henceforth, they accord themselves a political identity comparable to and distinguished from that of pagan Mecca as well as the nearby empires of Byzantium and Persia. There are 10 clauses devoted to what we would call 'social insurance' – the ransoming of captives, the payment of compensation, and general welfare: 'the believers shall have none of their members in destitution without giving him in kindness what he needs by way of ransom and blood money'.

The Constitution recognizes that people do not exist in a vacuum. Therefore, it acknowledges the existence of traditions, customs and pre-existing agreements and arrangements of the tribes in Medina and declares that they will 'keep to their tribal organisations and leadership, continuing to cooperate with each other in accordance with their former mutual aid agreements regarding blood money and related matters'. But it abolishes unjust practices such as the customary way of private justice, tribal vengeance, and excessive remuneration: 'a Muslim will not kill a Muslim in retaliation' nor will he 'demand an excessive sum of blood money or desire a gift of injustice, sin, transgression, or evil amongst the Muslims. They shall all unite against him even if he is the son of one of them.' There is no tribal responsibility, and hence no need for collective vengeance, for the act of an individual; each is solely responsible for his own actions: 'he who offends, offends only against himself' and 'charity and goodness are clearly distinguished from crime and injury, and there is no responsibility except for one's own deeds'. The administration of justice now becomes the concern of the central organization of the community of citizens.

▶ The citizens

The Constitution also gave due recognition to freedom of religion, particularly for the Jews, to whom it gives equal rights in all matters as citizens of Medina: 'the Jews have their religion and the Muslims have theirs'; 'any Jew who follows us is entitled to our assistance and the same rights as any one of us, without injustice and partisanship'; 'both enjoy the security of their own populace and clients except the unjust and criminals amongst them'; 'incumbent upon the Jews is their expenditure and upon the Muslims theirs'; and 'they will aid each other against whomsoever is at war with the people of this treaty'. Thus, differences in race and language are abolished. All are equal before the law of Medina and have equal rights. The members of all the groups within the community are asked to help each other, and cooperate and seek 'sincere advice and counsel' from each other.

There are also clauses relating to the defence of the city and what we might call a foreign policy. Finally, Medina is declared 'a sanctuary for the parties to this covenant'. The Constitution also establishes Muhammad as the leader of the community and the chief arbitrator of disputes among groups: 'whatever you differ about should be brought before Allah and Muhammad'.

All the Jewish clans who participated in the agreement are mentioned by name. There is some dispute as to whether this included all the Jews in Medina. The prevailing theory is that the document included all the inhabitants of Medina; this is certainly the view of Muslim, and many Western, scholars. However, contemporary Jewish scholars point out that the names of the three main Jewish clans of Medina – Nadir, Qurayza and Qaynuqa – are not mentioned in the document, although we do know that soon afterwards Muhammad concluded similar treaties with them. This apparent omission has been used to suggest that not all the Jews of Medina were party to the agreement. The counter argument is that the document mentions by name only the independent Jewish tribes, and not those that had client status. Those with client status are mentioned in general terms. Some tribes were closely identified with each other and hence are not specially named. There were also a number of unspecified pagan tribes not specially mentioned in the document. But that does not mean that they were excluded; they are described as *tabia* 'followers' or had 'become a client' of another tribe.

Collectively, the Muslims, Jews and pagans of Medina now constituted a single political community, with Muhammad as its leader. The document describes this new community as ummah – a word that has come to mean the global religious community composed exclusively of Muslims. But the Constitution of Medina was not a religious agreement. Not all the parties to the agreement had embraced Islam. They recognized the political authority of Muhammad and accepted him as a community leader, but many, as the document makes clear, were Jews and pagans.

> *This ummah was a community of common interests pursuing what they all recognized as the common good.*

The original significance of the term ummah was a multi-religious, one could even say multi-cultural, community committed to defending its joint interests.

The Believers

Muhammad and his early followers thought of themselves above all as being a *community of believers*, rather than one of Muslims, and referred to themselves as Believers . . . Some of the early Believers were Christians and Jews – although surely not all were. The reason for this 'confessionally open' or ecumenical quality is simply that the basic ideas of Believers and their insistence on observing strict piety were in no way antithetical to the beliefs and practices of some Christians and Jews.

Fred M Donner, *Muhammad and the Believers* (Harvard University Press, 2010; pp. 58, 69)

Muhammad was now acknowledged to be in a pre-eminent position, more powerful than the Jews and Christians of Medina. This was a serious cause of concern to the Jewish tribes. When a leading Rabbi, Abdullah bin Salam, converted to Islam, the Jews started a verbal campaign against Muhammad and Muslims. They tried to divide the Immigrants and the Helpers. A number of Rabbis and notables of the Jewish community tested the prophet on the faith of Abraham and tried to persuade him to move out of Medina and go to Jerusalem. Some Jews converted to Islam with the intention of subverting the faith from the inside. Muhammad tried to bring the three monotheistic faiths of the city together by organizing a conference for Christians, Jews and Muslims. Arguments were presented about the merits of the three faiths but, not surprisingly, no conclusions were reached. The Christians, however, agreed not to oppose Muhammad.

▲ Prophet's Mosque in Medina

Despite the Constitution of Medina, the city was not entirely at peace with itself. A revelation asked Muhammad to turn his face towards Mecca, rather than Jerusalem, during prayer: 'Many a time We have seen you [Prophet] turn your face towards Heaven, so We are turning you towards a prayer direction that pleases you. Turn your face in the direction of the Sacred Mosque: wherever you [believers] may be, turn your faces to it' (2: 144). This did not please the Jewish clans.

Meanwhile, Muhammad's erstwhile enemies in Mecca were fully aware of what was happening in Medina. The challenge Muhammad represented to their gods and pagan beliefs, and with it their vested interests in the riches they gained from their old way of life, was acquiring a new impetus. No longer constrained by the pressures of their opposition and persecution, Muhammad was liberated to advance the beliefs and practices of a monotheistic faith. There had already been several skirmishes between the Muslims and the Quraysh from Mecca. They were now ready to launch a full-scale assault on Medina.

7

The battles

ALL THAT
MATTERS

When he was in Mecca, Muhammad asked his followers to be patient and turn the other cheek in the face of adversity. Now, two years after the migration, he received regular reports that the Meccans were actively preparing to launch a major attack on Medina. He felt the urgency of preparing the nascent Muslim community to defend itself. A revelation gave him permission to take up arms against his enemies: 'Those who have been attacked are permitted to take up arms because they have been wronged – God has the power to help them – those who have been driven unjustly from their homes only for saying, "Our Lord is God" ' (22: 40).

During March in the year AD 624, Muhammad heard the news of a Meccan caravan of exceptional importance returning from Damascus. He knew that the goods and arms the caravan was bringing would increase the power and hence the threat posed by Mecca. He decided to intercept the caravan. The Meccans suspected this eventuality and were prepared. An army was despatched to protect the caravan, which, in the meantime, had diverted and managed to get beyond the reach of the Muslims. The Meccan force then pressed on towards Medina with the intention of attacking the city and eliminating the Muslims from Arabia.

Muhammad decided to confront the army of the Quraysh outside Medina, at the Bedouin hamlet of Badr, some 90 kilometres away. His army consisted of 313 ill-equipped men, 70 camels and two horses. The Quraysh force consisted of a thousand soldiers, 700 on camels and 300 on horseback, fully armed with shields, swords and arrows and other instruments of war. They took up their positions on higher ground and when they saw the small band of Muslims, on the morning of 17 March 624, they became impatient. 'Muhammad cannot escape us now,' they declared. The battle began, according to convention, with single combat: three Quraysh warriors came out and challenged the champions of the Muslims. All three were killed. Then, the armies charged at each other.

The battle itself was fierce but brief, lasting only a few hours. The discipline, passion and fury of the Muslims caught the Meccans off guard. Muhammad had asked his soldiers to seek out and attack the leaders of the Quraysh. One by one they fell. Panic broke in the Meccan ranks, and they started to run in different directions. At the end of the battle, 70 Meccans had died and 70 were captured.

The Battle of Badr was a decisive moment in the history of Islam. Defeat would have meant the eradication of the Muslims and history might have heard no more of them.

Their success at Badr established the Muslims as a force to be reckoned with. They had also done something unique. For the first time in the annals of Arabia an army based on faith, not on tribal or ethnic concerns, had defeated a far superior force.

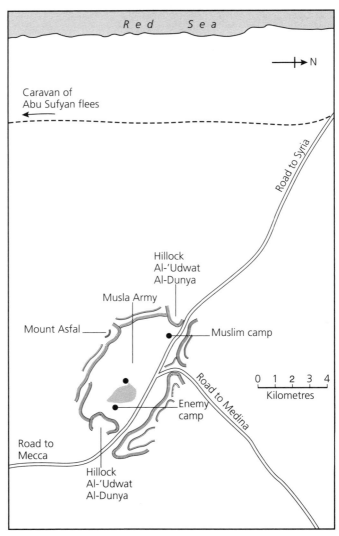

▲ **Map of the Battle of Badr**

Umayr's poem

Umayr bin al-Humam was eating some dates when the Meccans charged during the Battle of Badr. He threw his dates, seized his sword, and fought till he was slain – all the while singing the poem:

In God's service take no food
But piety and deed of good.
If in God's war you've firmly stood
You need not fear as others should
While you are righteous true and good.

(ibn Isahq, *The Life of Muhammad*, p. 300)

There was much debate and discussion amongst the Muslims about the fate of their prisoners. Muhammad consulted widely and wanted his followers to contribute freely towards making the decision. Some were of the opinion that the captives should be killed as a warning to others. Some thought they should be ransomed. Eventually, it was decided to ransom the prisoners and the necessary payments were set. Those who could not pay were asked instead to teach whatever they knew to young people in Medina. However, two prisoners were executed.

For the Meccans, their defeat spelled shame. It could not be forgotten or forgiven. It had to be avenged. The following year, the Meccans returned with an army of 3,000 warriors, 200 mounted, to avenge the honour of their city.

When Muhammad received news that the Meccans were about to march, he gathered the Muslims and Jews to discuss a tactical response. He favoured fortifying Medina and fighting the Quraysh within the city. Most of the young people were against being besieged and wanted to take the fight to the Quraysh outside the city. Finally, it was decided to meet the advancing force at Mount Uhad, a few kilometres outside Medina. Muhammad now had 700 men under arms.

At Uhad, Muhammad posted 50 archers at the mountain pass with strict orders not to move under any circumstances. When the Meccans approached they were forced back by showers of arrows. They were accompanied by their women. When their men tried to fall back, the women barred their way and urged them to go forward and fight. However, the continual showers of arrows broke the force of the Quraysh attack and they began to flee – women notwithstanding. The Muslims gave chase and captured their weapons and supplies. Thinking that the battle was over, the archers left their post.

Hind's song

Hind, the wife of the Quraysh leader Abu Safyan, accompanied her husband at the Battle of Uhad. Together with other women, she encouraged the Meccans to fight by playing the tambourine and singing:

On Ye sons of Abdul Dar,
On protectors of our rear,
Smite with every sharpened spear!
If you advance we hug you,
Spread soft rugs beneath you;
If you retreat we leave you,
Leave and no more love you.

(ibn Isahq, *The Life of Muhammad*, p. 374)

It was a fatal mistake. The Meccans saw their chance for a counterattack. A contingent circled around Mount Uhad and attacked the Muslims from the rear. At that point the fleeing Meccan forces turned back to renew their attack from the front. Suddenly the Muslims found themselves caught in a pincer movement. The formation of lines had gone and the Muslim force was confused. One by one the backbone of the Muslim army began to fall.

Even though 20 men were guarding Muhammad with their lives, he was struck down. Thought to be dead, his bodyguards began to carry him to the safety of the mountaintop. But it was only a glancing blow. His lip was cut and one of his lower teeth was broken. To the Muslims it seemed a miracle that the Prophet had survived. They gathered around Muhammad on the mountain top. By now the Quraysh were exhausted. Seeing that the Muslims had regrouped around Muhammad, they made no further attacks. With the Muslims secure on high ground and pelting them with stones, there was no way they could assail the hill.

The Meccans contented themselves with mutilating the bodies of Muslims who had fallen. Hind, the wife of the Quraysh leader Abu Sufyan, cut out the heart and liver of Muhammad's uncle, Hamza, and tried to chew them. Other women made strings of the ears, noses and other parts of the corpses and carried them to Mecca as souvenirs. Muslims suffered heavy losses, with 70 dead. The Quraysh lost 17 leaders.

Their success at Uhad emboldened the Quraysh of Mecca. Defeat encouraged the non-Muslim tribes of

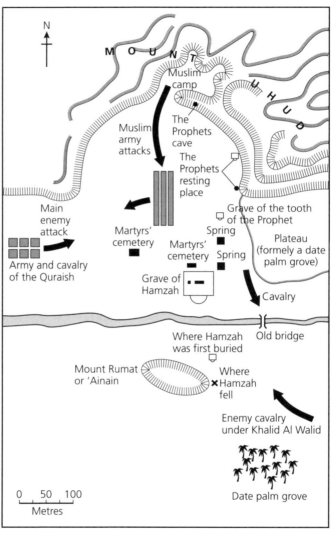

N

M O U N T

U H U D

Muslim camp

Muslim army attacks

The Prophets cave

The Prophets resting place

Main enemy attack

Army and cavalry of the Quraish

Martyrs' cemetery

Martyrs' cemetery

Grave of the tooth of the Prophet

Spring

Spring

Plateau (formely a date palm grove)

Grave of Hamzah

Cavalry

Old bridge

Where Hamzah was first buried

Mount Rumat or 'Ainain

Where Hamzah fell

Enemy cavalry under Khalid Al Walid

Date palm grove

0   50   100
Metres

▲ Map of the Battle of Uhad

Medina, who, only a few days earlier, had respected his authority, to openly oppose Muhammad. Some of the Jewish citizens were already fermenting trouble. After the victory of Badr, one of their leaders, Ka'b bin al-Ashraf, had gone to Mecca to form an alliance with the pagans and urge them to attack Mecca. After Uhad, they became openly hostile. The Jewish clan of Banu al-Nadir hatched a plot to assassinate Muhammad. The tribe was expelled from Medina; but was allowed to depart taking all their belongings, including armour. Indeed, they left the city with great pomp and splendour.

▶ Battle of the Trench

Muhammad's concerns were not just the trouble within Medina or his enemies in Mecca, who were eager to finish what they had started at Uhad.

All the tribes of Arabia were now openly hostile and conspiring against him.

He went out of his way to seek alliances and persuade as many tribes as he could to enter into peace treaties with him. In the Arab culture of the period, a major instrument for bringing tribes together was marriage. During this time Muhammad took a number of wives to cement such alliances.

The Meccans, too, were busy building alliances. They put together a mighty coalition based on meticulously negotiated alliances of most of the tribes of Arabia, instigated and funded by the Jewish clan of Banu al-Nadir, who had now settled in Khaybar. An army of over 10,000, from different parts of Arabia, converged on Medina. Arabia had never seen anything like it. Now it was the whole of Arabia against Muhammad.

As before, Muhammad consulted the citizens of Medina on methods of defending the city. A young Muslim, Salman the Persian, suggested an unusual ploy: the city was protected on one side by the houses of Medina, and on the other by high ground, so a trench should be dug between these points where Medina was open to the enemy. The suggestion was immediately accepted. Everyone, including Muhammad, participated in digging the trench, five yards deep and five yards wide. The Jewish tribe of Banu Quraiza, still in the city and allied to Muhammad, helped out with hoes and other equipment for digging the trench. The task was completed in six days. The length of the trench was divided into equal portions, with 10 archers assigned to defend each portion.

The coalition army reached Medina on 31 March 627. They arrived from the north and the south, descended 'from below the Muslims' and 'from above the Muslims' and camped in front of the city. They marched with swords drawn, arrows in their bows, drums beating and women shouting and singing. But they stopped at the trench. Camels would not go forward, horses reared back and the soldiers gasped at the sight of the trench. They had never seen anything like it. They tried their best but they could not get across the moat.

The Meccan army was well supplied with food and provisions. They decided to lay a siege to the city. Attempts were made to cross the moat. The few who succeeded were quickly picked off by the archers. For 30 days and 30 nights they attempted to cross the moat. The enthusiasm of the allied armies began to evaporate. Then the Jews of Bani Nader came up with a plan. They would ask their fellow Jews within Medina, the Banu Quraiza tribe, to revolt and attack Muhammad. Long negotiations between the two tribes took place; initially the leaders of Banu Quraiza were reluctant, but they eventually agreed. It did not take long for Muhammad to learn of the conspiracy. He reminded the Banu Quraiza of their mutual agreement. The Banu Quraiza declared: 'There is no agreement between us and Muhammad; and no pledge.'[24] The conversation ended in mutual abuse. The tribesmen of Banu Quraiza, who had been inside their fort during the siege, began to emerge and occupy the houses closer to the Muslim quarter in preparation for an attack.

Faced with an adversary within and a foe beyond the trench Muhammad decided to play off his enemies, one against the other. He sent a message to one of the major tribes of the alliance, promising one-third of the produce of Medina if they retreated and returned to their tribal home. A similar message was sent to another tribe. The allies became suspicious of each other and dissension broke out in their ranks.

Then nature intervened. The weather changed. A ferocious wind, combined with heavy rain, started. Lightning shattered the sky, as the wind tore apart the camp of the alliance. Confusion engulfed the allied forces. They decided to cut their losses and retreat. Rescuing as many of their belongings as they could, they returned to Mecca. The torrential rain and the strong wind continued till the Quraysh were a safe distance from Medina.

The external enemy had been repulsed. Muhammad now turned his attention to the Banu Quraiza, who had openly conspired with the allied forces to kill him and destroy the Muslim community. Their fort was besieged. The siege lasted 25 days, with fighting limited to throwing stones and shooting the occasional arrow. Eventually, the Banu Quraiza decided to surrender. They asked to be allowed to leave the city, with their belongings and armour, just as the Banu Nadir had done before. Muhammad refused.

What followed is regarded as one of the most controversial incidents of Muhammad's life. Muslim scholars argue that Banu Quraiza had signed a treaty not to assist his enemies, yet that is exactly what they did. According to the Constitution of Medina, they were traitors. Muhammad asked the Banu Quraiza to choose an arbitrator from among themselves: their fate would be determined by him. They chose Saad bin Maadh, a respectable man of the Jewish tribe of al Aws. Before undertaking to arbitrate, Saad took an oath from both sides that they would abide by his decision. When both sides agreed, he gave his verdict: 'I give judgement that the men should be killed, the property divided, and women and children taken as captive.'[25] The harsh sentence was carried out.

Why did Saad condemn Banu Quraiza to such a horrible fate? Clearly the Banu Quraiza did not expect a man of their own choosing to pass such a judgement. It might have occurred to Saad that, if the Banu Quraiza had succeeded in their plot, the Muslims would have met a similar fate at the hands of the Quraysh and their allies. He therefore imposed on them the fate to which they wished to subject the Muslims. If they had been spared, they might, like other Jewish tribes including Bani Nader, go and join the enemies of the Muslims, thus strengthening their ranks. Traditional accounts also suggest that Saad had been seriously wounded by the allies of Banu Quraiza during the defence of Medina, that he could not walk and had to be carried to the place of arbitration. He had also suffered abuse at the hands of Banu Quraiza during the Battle of the Trench. Therefore, he could well have had a personal grudge against them.

The incident is in sharp contrast to Muhammad's earlier treatment of Jews in Medina. This is why some Muslim scholars have argued that the event never actually occurred and contend that the sources have embellished the incident. This line of reasoning is supported by the suggestion that Muhammad took a captive, a woman called Rayhana, in a diplomatic marriage. What good would such a gesture be if Muhammad had actually destroyed the Banu Qurayza? Most Western scholars accept the conventional narrative and describe the execution of the Banu Qurayza as a barbaric act unworthy of a prophet and religious leader. This line of reasoning rests on a very specific ideal of prophethood that is asserted irrespective of context and circumstance. It ignores the numerous battles and acts of violence recorded for various Old Testament prophets. Indeed, it owes a great deal to a concept of prophethood honoured more in the breach throughout history but which has gathering appeal to modern sensibilities, if not modern practice. Certainly, it was a product of escalating tensions between Muhammad and the Jews of Medina, leading to a military confrontation. Yet, it cannot be seen, as some would have it, as evidence of an anti-Jewish policy, either at the time or in setting a pattern for the course of Muslim history. Rather grimly, it has also been suggested that the incident reflects 'the politics of mercy'.

For by the inescapable logic of human nature, mercy is only really appreciated if it has first been combined with fear. If the Prophet had not revealed at least one incident of implacable judgement the clemency that he would later show [at Mecca, for instance] could have been mistaken as a weakness.[26]

The fate of the Banu Quraiza did not end the Jewish presence in Medina. Some Jewish clans remained in the city. Jewish resistance to Muhammad continued elsewhere in Arabia, directed from their strongly fortified city of Khayber.

8

Hudaibya and Khayber

A number of pagan tribes that were settled in the region around Medina participated in the allied onslaught on the city. Muhammad spent most of the year following the Battle of the Trench dealing with them. A small expedition was sent to the town of Dhu-Qarad; its inhabitants were engaged in raiding and kidnapping Muslims from Medina. Another small force, of around 200 men, was sent to Fidak, where a new plan was being hatched to invade Medina. But Muhammad's own mind was elsewhere.

In February AD 628, he gave advanced warning that he intended to go to Mecca – as a pilgrim. He donned the simple dress of a pilgrim and set off for the city of his birth to visit the Kaaba. He was accompanied by 1,400 of his followers, all dressed in ritualistic pilgrim garb – two unsown pieces of white cloth, one serving as a loin cloth, the other wrapped toga-like covering one shoulder – and carrying no weapons. All were going to perform *umra*, the lesser pilgrimage.

Naturally, the Quraysh were none too pleased to hear of Muhammad's intended visit to Mecca. They suspected his motives. Was it a new tactic? A war game designed to enter and subdue Mecca? They thought it was a manoeuvre designed to show the world that, while the Quraysh could not gain entry to Medina, Muhammad could enter Mecca. They swore to prevent Muhammad on any account. A party of 200 riders was dispatched to intercept Muhammad's convey and prevent him reaching the city.

Muhammad's pilgrims' caravan was forced to stop at Hudaibiya, about 12 kilometres from Mecca. The Quraysh sent men to the Muslim camp, both on fact-finding missions and to warn Muhammad. One of them was Urwa bin Masud, a well-travelled old man considered to be wise. He came and sat before Muhammad. His language was not particularly diplomatic, and every time he spoke his hand almost touched Muhammad's beard. The Prophet's companions were concerned and there were sharp exchanges. Muhammad assured Urwa that he had not come to fight but only to perform the umra. When Urwa returned to Mecca he informed the Quraysh how Muhammad's companions treated him: 'I have seen Khusraw in his kingdom and Caesar in his kingdom and the Negus in his kingdom, but never have I seen a king among a people like Muhammad is among his companions.'[27] For a time, it looked as if a stalemate had been reached. Muhammad sent messengers of his own to the leaders of the Quraysh. They were treated harshly. A small party of Quraysh raided the Muslim camp at night and pelted them with stones. The Meccans tried to provoke Muhammad to fight – knowing that without any weapons the Muslims were in no position to defend themselves. Then, they sent a special envoy to negotiate.

Insulting Muhammad

Muhammad was frequently mocked and abused. This is mentioned in the Qur'an: 'Whenever they see you O Prophet they ridicule you' (24: 41) and 'the disbelievers think it strange that a prophet of their own people has come to warn them: they say, "he is just a lying sorcerer" ' (38: 4). These attacks must have upset him. But the Qur'an advises him to 'have patience with what they say, and leave them with noble dignity' (73: 10). He is repeatedly asked to 'forgive and overlook' (5: 13) and to treat those who abuse him with kindness. Thus, despite contemporary claims, there is no law against blaspheming Muhammad.

His name was Sohail bin Amr, one of Mecca's most articulate and influential men. He came with a proposal. This time Muhammad was to return to Medina without entering Mecca; the following year he would be allowed to enter Mecca for three days to perform the pilgrimage. By this arrangement, they argued, the Arabian tribes would not be able to claim that Muhammad entered Mecca in defiance of the Quraysh. After some discussion, and the usual consultations, Muhammad accepted the proposal.

The negotiations, however, were still not concluded. The agreement had to be committed to writing. It was part of the Qur'anic revelation that transparent and open dealing between parties to an agreement should be recorded in writing. What followed demonstrates how accommodating and flexible Muhammad was prepared to be; and how determined he was to make peace.

Muhammad dictated the words 'In the name of God, the Beneficent'. But Sohail objected. He knew nothing of this Beneficent God. He insisted on using the customary formula: 'In your name, O Allah.' The Muslims murmured, but Muhammad accepted. He went on to dictate: 'This is the treaty of peace between the Prophet of God . . .' Sohail objected again. To acknowledge that Muhammad was the Prophet of God would be tantamount to becoming his follower. The designation should simply be 'Muhammad bin Abdullah'. This time the Muslims were really agitated. They refused to change the sentence. Some of them held the hand of the scribe and declared that 'Muhammad the Prophet of God' must be written or the matter settled in a battle. Muhammad himself called for the words 'the Prophet of God' to be pointed out to him, crossed them out and instructed his cousin, Ali, to write Muhammad ibn Abdullah.[28] The writing of the treaty proceeded without further interruptions: it specified that peace was to last for 10 years and that any person from the Quraysh migrating to Muhammad's camp in Medina would be returned to Mecca, but any Muslim emigrating from Medina to Mecca would not be returned. It also stipulated that local tribes were free to ally themselves to either the Quraysh or Muhammad without hindrance from either side.

As soon as the Treaty of Hudaibya was concluded, various tribes started to declare which side they would support. The clan of Banu Bakr, Muhammad's old and inveterate enemies, joined the Quraysh. The Khuza joined Muhammad. Sohail's son, Abu Jandal, announced that he was joining the Muslim camp. Sohail was incensed at seeing his son change loyalties in his presence. He punched his son in the face, and pulled him by his hair back to the Quraysh camp. Abu Jandal called out to the Muslims to save him from being returned to Mecca and persecuted for his faith. The Muslims felt compelled to act. But Muhammad told Abu Jandal to 'have patience and be disciplined for God will soon provide a way out for you and your persecuted friends from your suffering. We have entered with the Quraysh into a treaty of peace and we have exchanged with them a solemn pledge that none will cheat the other.'[29] Abu Jandal was taken back in custody to Mecca.

The Muslims were disheartened. They returned to Medina thinking they had been humiliated.

> ## On the surface, the Treaty of Hudaibya appears rather one-sided.

But even before the Muslims reached Medina, a revelation declared the Hudaibiya agreement to be a victory:

> *Truly We have opened up a path to clear triumph for you, so that God may forgive you your past and future sins, complete His grace upon you and guide you to the straight path, and help you mightily.*

> *(48: 1–3)*

The verses were a reminder that a truce, even if it appears one-sided, even if it brings only partial peace, is to be preferred. Indeed, the treaty did bring peace to Medina and provided Muhammad with much-needed breathing space. Hostility between Mecca and Medina was replaced with security and mutual trust. Conversions to Islam increased manifold.

▶ The Khaybar expedition

The Hudaibya agreement considerably reduced the Jewish influence on Arabia. The Jewish clans based in Khaybar were among the richest and strongest people in the peninsula. Their fort was exceptionally well protected and equipped for all eventualities. With the Quraysh out of the picture, their power was somewhat diminished. They suspected that Muhammad would move against them. Some of their leaders were of the opinion that alliances should be made with other Jewish tribes in Arabia and a pre-emptive strike made against Medina. Other leaders wished to enter into a Hudaibya-type treaty. While the Jewish clans were still debating their next move, Muhammad decided to march against Khaybar. He led an army of 1,600 battle-hardened soldiers, with a cavalry of 100. They moved swiftly and clandestinely to reach Khaybar within three days. The Jewish tribes were taken by surprise. They only learned of Muhammad's army when it was standing in front of their city. It was the morning of 15 March 628.

Muhammad's orders to his army

Do not kill women, children and non-combatants, or cut down trees or destroy buildings.

The Quraysh and other tribes of Arabia, including the neutral Jewish tribe of Ghatafan, watched the campaign from the sidelines and awaited the outcome. The Jewish tribes of Khaybar realized that this was their last stand against Muhammad. The city had six different forts and several fortified quarters. The Jewish clans stored their treasures in one fort and their families in another, while the warriors took shelter in a third, called Natat. It was a good strategy; Muhammad's army could not lay siege to all the forts at once. Nor could he maintain his position for long; he did not have provisions for a prolonged war and there was every chance he might be cut off from Medina. Muhammad attacked Natat and a fierce battle took place. The Jews fought bravely, 50 Muslims were wounded and Muhammad had to retreat.

The siege, however, continued. Further attempts were made to capture Natat. Finally, Ali, the cousin of the Prophet, managed to break in. The defenders immediately moved to the next fort, Qamus. This was also taken. They moved to the next, al-Saab. By now the provisions of Muhammad's army had run out and they had to eat their horses to survive.

> *There was strenuous fighting to capture al-Saab, with the Jews fighting heroically in its defence.*

But it too was captured. Al-Saab had plenty of food and water so Muhammad's army finally had all the provisions it needed. Having relieved their hunger, the Muslims turned their attention to the next fort.

The Jews had now gathered in the fortress of al Zubayr. It was surrounded and attacked a number of times.

Courageously defended, the Muslims could not take the fort – until they discovered and seized its water supply. The Jews were forced to come out and engage the Muslims in open battle. They lost. The remaining forts fell quickly till only the fortresses of Watih and Sulaim were left. This is where the defenders' families were hiding and their treasures were stored. The Jews now became desperate and offered to surrender on specific terms: their lives should be spared, their women and children should not be touched, and in return they would pay half the produce of their land in homage to Medina. Their terms were accepted. The news of the fall of Khabar spread quickly. Other Jewish clans, including those based in Fadak, Wadi al Qura and Tayma, also accepted the authority of Muhammad.

▶ Letters and emissaries

The relationship between Jews and Muslims did not immediately become peaceful. Their defeat at Khaybar stirred resentment on the Jewish side. There was even an attempt to poison Muhammad. Eventually, the region north of Medina was rendered as calm as the south had been, thanks to the Hudaibya agreement. It was during this period that Muhammad sent letters to the rulers and kings of adjoining countries inviting them to join the faith of Islam. He sent letters to Heraclius of Byzantium, who ruled the empire from the city of Antioch; Chosroes II of the Persian Empire; the ruler of Alexandria; the lords of Syria; and the Negus of Abyssinia. The letters were similar, each short, direct and worded appropriately for each recipient. To Heraclius, for example, Muhammad wrote:

> In the name of God, the Merciful and Compassionate. From Muhammad, the Messenger of God, to Heraclius, the ruler of Romans. Peace to whoever follows the right guidance. To proceed: Submit yourself, and you shall be safe. Submit yourself, and God shall give you reward twice over. But, if you turn away, the sin of the Husbandmen shall be upon you.[30]

The sin of the Husbandmen may be a reference to the parable of wicked Husbandman in Matthew 22: 33–46. To the Negus, Muhammad wrote:

> In the name of God, the Merciful and Compassionate. From Muhammad, the Messenger of God, to the Negus al-Asham, king of the Ethiopians. May you be at peace! I praise to you God, the King, the Most Holy, the Peace, the Keeper of Faith, the Watcher, and I bear witness that Jesus the son of Mary is the Spirit and Word of God, which he cast into the goodly and chaste Virgin Mary, so that she conceived Jesus, whom God created from His Spirit and breathed into him, even as He created Adam by His hand and breathed into him. I call you to God alone, Who has no partner, to continued obedience to Him, and that you follow me and believe in what has come to me; for I am the Messenger of God.[31]

The following year, as stipulated in the Hudaibya agreement, Muhammad went to Mecca for umra, the lesser pilgrimage. He was accompanied by 2,000 companions, many of them Muhajirs who had not seen their birthplace or the families they had left behind for seven years. The Quraysh kept their side of the bargain and left the city with their families. After three days, the Muslims were asked to leave the city. They obliged, but by now a number of notable Meccans, including Khalid bin Walid, the Quraysh's hero of the Battle of Uhad, had converted to Islam and accompanied Muhammad to Medina.

In the coming months, Muhammad sent a number of missionaries throughout Arabia, inviting various tribes and clans to Islam. Many of these ambassadors were killed. He also sent an expedition to Syria. Historians differ about the reasons for this campaign. Some suggest that it was initiated at the murder of his emissary to the Byzantine governor of Basra. Others give the murder of one of his companions as the cause. Whatever the reason, Heraclius was well prepared. Some accounts suggest that he led his army himself; others that his brother, Theodorus, was its commander. Muhammad's army of 3,000 met an army estimated between 100,000 and 200,000 Greek and Arab soldiers at the Battle of Mutah. As one Muslim commander after another fell during the battle, and Muslim ranks became disorganized, command finally fell on the shoulders of Khalid bin Walid. Using his experience of the Battle of Uhad, he employed a similar tactic to fox the enemy. A contingent was deployed towards the rear of the enemy to give the impression that massive reinforcements had arrived from Medina to join the battle. The strategy worked. The Syrian army, already convinced of the determination with which the Muslims fought, decided to abandon the battle and withdrew. The Muslims returned to Medina, neither victorious nor defeated.

The Quraysh viewed the outcome of the Battle of Mutah quite differently. They were of the opinion that Muslim power and dignity were now compromised. Muhammad could still be defeated. In the clear violation of the Hudaibya agreement, Banu Bakr, encouraged by the Quraysh, attacked the Khuza, a tribe allied with the Muslims, to settle old scores. While the members of Khuza were sleeping in a place near Mecca, Banu Bakr fell on them, killing some and looting their property. The Khuza took shelter in Mecca but received no protection from the Quraysh. They ran to Medina and reported what had happened to Muhammad. The Prophet asked the Quraysh to pay compensation to the Khuza and desist from helping and supporting Banu Bakr or to declare the Hudaibya agreement null and void.

The Quraysh chose the second option. Muhammad asked his followers to mobilize themselves in defence of the Khuza. His objective, however, was larger than defending the terms of the Treaty of Hudaibya.

9

The triumph of forgiveness

ALL THAT MATTERS

Almost immediately after dissolving the Hudaibya agreement, the Quraysh began to have doubts. They sent Abu Sufyan, the most prominent leader of Mecca, to speak to Muhammad and attempt to renew the treaty. He was refused an audience. He asked Abu Bakr, Muhammad's closest companion, to intercede on his behalf. Abu Bakr refused. He went to Ali and Fatima, the Prophet's son-in-law and daughter, but was again turned down. Finally, Abu Sufyan went to the Mosque in Medina and proclaimed that Meccans were willing to make peace. He then returned to Mecca.

As the Muslims prepared for mobilization, they thought they were on their way to Syria to conclude the unfinished business of the Battle of Mutah. Some, however, knew or guessed what was about to happen. A prominent Muslim, Hatib bin Abi Balta, who had fought at the Battle of Badr, send a secret message to Mecca warning them of an impending invasion. Hatib was concerned about the fate of his own family and children, as well as his clan, who were with the Quraysh in Mecca. The letter was intercepted, but Hatib's treason was forgiven.

Muhammad's preparations were so well organized, and his advance towards Mecca so rapid, that the Quraysh were taken by surprise. They learned of the Muslim advance only when it was less than half a day's journey from Mecca. The Muslim army reached Mecca in January AD 630; it was 10,000 strong and well equipped. It consisted of many tribes, each with its own leader and its own camp. Muhammad asked them to spread out and make huge bonfires in front of their camps. A few Meccans, including

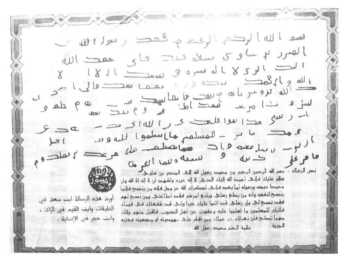

▲ Letter attributed to Muhammad, bearing his seal

Abu Safyan, made a clandestine foray to estimate the size of the Muslim army. They were astonished to see how far the Muslim forces were spread. But their presence was detected and they were caught. This time Abu Safyan was granted an audience with Muhammad.

When Abu Safyan was brought to Muhammad, he found himself in front of a court consisting of the elders of the Muhajirun and the Ansar. There was heated discussion and many wished to see Abu Safyan executed. However, after a dialogue between Muhammad and Abu Safyan, this long-term redoubtable opponent converted to Islam. As a leader of the Quraysh and a proud man, he expected some privileges, which were granted. Muhammad announced that whoever entered the house of Abu Safyan would be safe. Those who remained in their houses and locked their doors would be safe. And those who congregated around the Kaaba would be safe.

Scholars disagree whether Abu Safyan came to Muhammad by accident, or whether this was a pre-arranged meeting. There is little doubt that Abu Safyan had genuinely converted to Islam. The following morning, the Muslim armies entered Mecca unopposed. The army was divided into four divisions, with strict orders not to fight or shed any blood. Abu Safyan ran through the streets of Mecca calling on his people to offer no resistance. But a handful of Meccans, belonging to the Banu Bakr clan, who had violated the Hudaibya agreement still resisted, and there was a skirmish involving Khalid bin Walid's battalion. Calm was soon restored.

Muhammad now went to the Kaaba and performed the *tawaf*: he went around the Kaaba seven times, a ritual that symbolizes the unity of believers in the worship of One God. The Meccans gathered around the Prophet, and he delivered an address:

> There is no god but God. He has no associate. He has made good His promise and helped His servant. He has put to flight the allied army [during the Battle of the Trench]. Every claim of privilege [inherited authority] or blood [on account of tribal feuds] or property are abolished by me . . . O Quraysh God has taken you from the haughtiness of paganism and veneration of ancestors. Man springs from Adam and Adam sprang from dust.[32]

Then he read the following verse of the Qur'an:

> *People, We created you out from a single man and a single woman and made you into races and tribes so that you should recognise one another (and not despise each other). In God's eyes, the most honoured of you are the ones most mindful of Him.*
>
> *(49: 13)*

After he finished his address, Muhammad looked at the Quraysh. There in the gathering were those who persecuted him, tortured and killed his followers, conspired to murder him, drove him out of his city of birth, incited the tribes of Arabia to rise against him, and waged relentless wars to destroy him and his people.

'O people of Quraysh,' he asked, 'What do you think I am going to do to you?' They replied in unison: 'Good. You are a noble brother, son of a noble brother.' Muhammad replied, 'There is no blame on you this day. You are free to go your way.'[33]

He then entered the Kaaba. Its walls were painted with pictures. He asked that pictures and images be removed. It also contained a number of idols, with Hubal, the chief deity, carved in precious stone, at the centre. The Prophet touched all of them, one by one, with his stick and recited the verse: 'Say, the Truth has come and falsehood has passed away: falsehood is bound to pass away' (17: 81). The idols were then torn down and smashed.

Mecca was declared a sacred and holy city. Muhammad ordered that it was forbidden to shed blood in the city or to destroy any tree in and around Mecca. All killing must stop, he announced, for it is an evil crime. The general amnesty, a profound act of forgiveness, had a deep impact on the inhabitants of Mecca. They queued up to be converted and the whole city embraced Islam.

▶ The Hunain encounter

The conquest of Mecca, however, did not end the hostilities of the pagan tribes of Arabia. In particular, the tribes of Hawazin and Thaqif, which had been strong supporters of the Quraysh, were bitterly opposed to Muhammad. Hawazin, a powerful, violent tribe, lived between Mecca and Taif. Thaqif were the ruling tribe of Taif, where Muhammad was stoned and thrown out when he went to preach while he was still based in Mecca. Taif was also the site of the temple of Al-Lat, one of the chief deities of the pagans. Had Muhammad not taken Mecca by surprise, the Hawazin and Thaqif would have joined the Quraysh to defend it. As Muhammad was converting the inhabitants of Mecca, the Hawazin and Thaqif were getting ready to make war against him. They managed to bring other tribes together to form a joint front to oppose the Muslims. They mobilized all their members, including women and children, and carried all their possessions to the battlefield. They planned their campaign very carefully before marching to the valley of Hunain, to the southeast of Mecca. The plan was simple: as the Muslims marched through the valley, they would be attacked in the dark with arrows. When the Muslims retreated in disarray, the pagan tribes would fall upon them as one man, and reduce the Muslim ranks into rabble. The Muslims would be defeated decisively, and their victory over Mecca would become irrelevant. It was a plan that Muhammad himself had used in the Battle of Uhad. And it almost worked.

Ansar concern

The Ansar, Muhammad's long-time supporters who had accompanied him from Medina, were concerned that the Prophet would resettle in Mecca. On hearing of their fears, Muhammad assured them that he would live and die in Medina. He stayed in Mecca for only two weeks before returning to Medina.

Muhammad heard of the preparations of the Hawazin and Thaqif towards the end of his short stay in Mecca. He set out to meet them with a force of 12,000 soldiers – 10,000 of whom had come with him from Medina, and 2,000 of whom were new converts from Mecca, including Abu Safyan. His army passed the valley of Hunain while it was still dark. As planned, it was greeted with a shower of arrows. Unable to see the enemy, the Muslim army retreated. A general charge followed; tribesmen of Hawazin and Thaqif poured down from the sides of the canyon in vast numbers with their long spears. Panic stricken, the Muslims began to run in all directions.

But Muhammad stood his ground. He was surrounded by some of his closest companions. A call went out for the Muslims to regroup. By now the whole of the pagan camp had descended from their vantage points on the hill and were face to face with Muhammad's army. The sun had appeared over the horizon. 'Rally forth to battle,' chanted the Muslims as they quickly reorganized their ranks. Muhammad watched as men began to fall on both sides. Soon, the Hawazin, Thaqif and their allies realized that victory was not possible and began to flee. They left their women, children, camels, sheep and silver behind. Around 6,000 were captured. But Muhammad did not let his enemy rest. He moved to Taif and laid siege to the city. It was unsuccessful and, after a month, he returned to Medina.

By now, Muhammad, aged 60, was a powerful leader of a rapidly growing community. Islam was the dominant and most powerful force in Arabia. Emissaries began to arrive from all over Arabia, offering peace and, in some cases, expressing the desire to 'enter the religion of God'. Conversion was not just a matter of accepting that there is only one God and Muhammad is His Messenger: it also required the payment of zakat, the compulsory religious tax that is the due and the right of the poor, as well as *sadaqa*, voluntary charity. Those who did not embrace Islam became clients of the

Muslim state. The people of Taif were among the first to send their emissaries and willingly converted to Islam. The delegation of Banu Tamim, a tribe from eastern Arabia, arrived in Medina and challenged Muhammad to a poetic duel. Their poets spoke of their noble character and exalted status. The reply came from two of Muhammad's companions who spoke of 'the nobility of people who have God's apostle with them'. After the competition the Banu Tamim declared their faith in Islam. The delegation from Najran, a Christian town between Mecca and Yemen, consisted largely of priests. They were allowed to worship in the Prophet's mosque. They questioned Muhammad about Jesus, but they were not satisfied with his answers. Muhammad asked them to join him in a prayer, reciting verses of the Qur'an: 'Come, let us gather our sons and your sons, our women and your women, ourselves and yourselves, and let us pray earnestly and invoke God's rejection on those of us who are lying' (3: 61). They refused. Then Muhammad asked them to join him in a monotheistic fellowship, reciting the verse: 'Say, People of the Book, let us arrive at a statement that is common to us all: we worship God alone, we ascribe no partner to Him, and none of us takes others besides God as lords' (3: 64). They agreed, but then changed their minds and returned to Najran. Delegation followed delegation, and virtually all of the year beginning April 630 was spent receiving emissaries. Hence, this 10th year after the migration to Medina is known in Muslim tradition as 'the year of deputations'.

▶ Farewell Sermon

By this time virtually all the pagan tribes of Arabia had become Muslim, and those who still remained Christians and Jews came under Muhammad's protection. Muhammad himself was physically and mentally exhausted. The battles, the constant concerns for his followers, family tragedies as well as constant prayer and fasting had taken their toll. His mission to unite Arabia under the banner of Islam was almost complete. In just over two decades, he had transformed the feuding and undisciplined Arabs into an organized and disciplined society. He had provided them with a vision of a just society and, even though he himself could not read or write, he had infused a strong love of knowledge and learning among his followers. In short, he had laid the foundations for a vibrant culture and civilization. Only one longing remained: to perform the hajj, the full version of the pilgrimage to Mecca.

Muhammad's prayer

O Lord! Let me live among the poor, let me die among the poor; and on the day of resurrection raise me among the poor.

During February 632, Muhammad was finally able to fulfil his ardent desire, 10 years after he had been forced to migrate from his native city. He led a convoy, said to be between 90,000 and 120,000 pilgrims, from Medina to Mecca. It came to be known as his 'Farewell Pilgrimage'. Towards the end of the pilgrimage, he delivered a sermon at Arafat, one of the ritual sites of hajj, a short distance from Mecca. Sitting on his camel, he spoke to a vast crowd, his words taken up by individuals placed at key positions and relayed to the assembly.

In the Farewell Sermon, Muhammad reminds Muslims of the five pillars of their faith – belief in One God and His Messenger, prayer, fasting, charity and the pilgrimage to Mecca – and gives a full account of how the hajj is to be performed. Then he summarizes his life's teachings with these words:

> *O people, lend me an attentive ear for I know not whether, after this year, I shall be amongst you.*
> *Regard the life and property of every Muslim as a sacred trust.*
> *Return the goods entrusted to you to their rightful owners.*
> *Hurt no one so that no one may hurt you.*
> *Do not take usury; this is forbidden to you. Aid the poor and clothe them as you would clothe yourselves.*
> *It is true that you have certain rights with regards to your wives but they also have rights over you. Treat them well and be kind to them for they are your partners and helpers.*
> *Know that every Muslim is a Muslim's brother, and that the Muslims are brethren.*
> *It is only lawful to take from a brother what he gives you willingly.*
> *Do not do injustice to your own selves.*

No one is higher than the other unless he is higher in virtue. Reason well, and ponder my words which I now convey to you.[34]

When he had finished his sermon, he asked: 'O God! Have I conveyed my message?' The crowd replied in unison: 'Yes.' The following verse was then revealed: 'Today I have perfected your religion for you, completed My blessings upon you, and chosen as your religion Islam' (5: 3).

Muhammad did not live long after this sermon. He became ill, suffering from fever and headache, and could not sleep at night. He died in June 632, at the age of 63, surrounded by his family and companions. He was buried in a room in the house of his wife Aisha.

Within the next 50 years, Muhammad's followers held sway from Persia to Egypt, had a strong presence in the Mediterranean and were on their way to Spain. Within a century, Islam had become a global religion and a flourishing civilization.

10

Wives and warfare

Details of the life of Muhammad the man were central to the institutionalizing of Islam as religion and the shaping of the customs and conventions of the daily life of Muslims. It is hardly surprising, then, that the character of Muhammad should be central to the criticism of Islam that arose in the Western Christian world. From the earliest report of the new religion written by John of Damascus (AD 645/676–749), an official in the court of the Muslim Caliph Yazid II, to eighteenth-century Enlightenment thinkers and nineteenth-century Orientalists such as William Muir[35] and Father Henri Lammens,[36] this critique has had two consistent themes: warfare and wives.

For example, two luminaries of the Enlightenment, Voltaire and Volney, described Muhammad in all the colours of darkness. For Voltaire, Muhammad was a 'false prophet' who founded a barbaric cult.[37] In his novel *Les Ruines*, C F Volney portrays Muhammad as a violent leader determined to 'subdue with the sabre those who refuse to believe in his law'.[38] Similarly, because of his multiple marriages, Muhammad was depicted as a licentious man. Much of this criticism has resurfaced in the twenty-first century from the more extreme wing of 'neo-conservative' writers.

Western scholars are hardly in a position to throw such criticism at Muhammad when we consider Christianity's record on wars and violence and the West's own history. But one can ask a more pertinent question: given the circumstances of time and place, is it conceivable that Muhammad's mission could have been accomplished without his battles? In the early part of his mission, as we have seen, Muhammad certainly avoided conflict as much as possible. His community had neither the strength nor resources to do otherwise. After the hijra it is evident that a military option was adopted.

The mental images conjured by the language of 'war' and 'battles' for a modern reader is perhaps not the best way to think about the kind of clashes that took place in Muhammad's time.

Both the battles of Badr and Uhad lasted less than a day, and the battle did not even take place at the Battle of the Trench. The longest period Muhammad himself was engaged in military encounter was the siege of Khyaber. Thus, in a period of 23 years, during which he was a prophet, Muhammad spent only a few months engaged in fighting.

There were many other raids and clashes involving Muhammad's followers. The classical sources make no secret of these minor encounters with the enemies who sought the obliteration of the nascent Muslim community. Indeed, the entire genre of biography of the Prophet began as works recording these skirmishes. Arabia was a society and culture deeply wedded to the code of the warrior where raiding, looting and plundering were endemic. To survive, the Muslims had to defend and fight. The important caveat is that the Qur'an contains a clear ethic, a kind of just war theory inclusive of a Geneva Convention on the rules of war. These make clear that war must only be defensive in nature: civilians, women, children and the elderly could not be attacked; places of worship of whatever kind – church, synagogue, temple or mosque – could not be ransacked; and animals, water sources and crops could not be destroyed. Furthermore, if the enemy asks for peace the offer must be accepted immediately. Muslims have fared no worse than followers of other prophets; and at times they have fared much better in pursuit of peace, tolerance and living together with peoples of other faiths and cultures.

The matter of Muhammad's marriages also has to be taken in context. Marriage is the lubricant of a society based on kinship, such as the tribal society of seventh-century Arabia. Indeed, marriage has been the means of creating and cementing relationships among rulers and leaders of innumerable societies of vastly different kinds up until very recent times. It should not surprise us, then, that most of Muhammad's marriages had a political context.

Muhammad married 11 women in all. But for most of his life, he was monogamous, married to his first wife, Khadijah, for 25 years. After the death of Khadijah in 619, and while still in Mecca, he married Sawdah bint Zam'a, a recent widow, and Aisha, the daughter of his closest companion, Abu Bakr. Eight of his marriages occurred after he arrived in Medina and became the leader of the community. In addition, he also had a concubine: Maria al Qibtiyya, a Coptic Christian Egyptian sent as a gift by a Byzantine official. She is the only one of Muhammad's wives, apart from Khadijah, who bore him a child. Their son Ibrahim died in infancy. And there was Rayhana bint Zayd, captured after the defeat of Banu Qurazya. Classical sources differ over whether she was a concubine or eventually married him. Together, they are known as 'Mothers of the Believers'.

Mothers of the Believers

Khadija bint Khuwaylid
Sawda bint Zam'a
Aisha bint Abu Bakr
Hafsa bint Umar
Zaynab bint Khuzayma
Hind bint Abu Umayya
Zaynab bint Jahsh
Juwayriyya bint al-Harith
Rayhana bint Zayd
Safiyya bint Huyayy
Ramla bint Abu Safyan
Maria al-Qibtiyya
Maymuna bint al-Harith

The earlier marriages aimed at cementing relationships with the core group of Muhammad and its adherents. Muhammad married his own daughters to his companions. Ruqayyah and Umm Kulthum both married Uthman. Fatima was married to her cousin Ali, one of the strongest supporters of Muhammad. Apart from Aisha, Muhammad also married Hafsah, the widowed 18-year-old daughter of Umar. Abu Bakr, Umar, Uthman and Ali were all among Muhammad's closest and most important companions and would each in turn become Caliph, literally successor to Muhammad, as the leader of the Muslim community. These marriages constituted the glue that bound his companions to Muhammad.

The later marriages cemented tribal alliances or served as a rationale for reconciliation. For example, Jawayriyya bint al Harith was taken captive in the skirmish with the Banu Mustaliq, during which her husband was killed. When Muhammad married her, and it became known that people of the Mustaliq clan were now kinsmen of the Prophet, other Muslims immediately released their captives. Ramla, or Umm Habiba, was the daughter of Abu Sufyan, a leader of the Meccan elite so fiercely opposed to Muhammad. This marriage was an alliance with one of the most influential citizens of Mecca.

Two of Muhammad's marriages have become quite controversial. The first is with Aisha, whom he married when she was said to be 9 or 10 and he was 53. Conventions about the age of marriage are culturally determined and have changed radically over time. Child marriage and considerable age difference were no impediment within the cultural context of seventh-century Arabian society. Women were able to be married immediately after beginning menstruation, a sign of maturation that has been the threshold in most societies throughout much of human history. Should a prophet have been an example of how society and its sensibilities would change over millennia? Is it proper to apply contemporary sensibilities, the modern construction of childhood, to persons who lived in entirely different circumstances? It is worth noting that criticism of this marriage has appeared only in modern times. What is abundantly clear from the sources is that such a marriage, not consummated until Aisha had achieved what was regarded as maturity, caused no comment in Mecca at that time – or in the Christendom of the Middle Ages.

The second marriage, with Zaynab bint Jahsh, who was Muhammad's cousin, did raise eyebrows in Arabia. It is the only marriage to be specifically mentioned in the Qur'an. Zaynab was married to Zaid, Muhammad's adopted son. But Zaynab was not happy; and her brothers too rejected Zaid because they were of an aristocratic lineage while he had been a slave. Muhammad intervened to urge them not to divorce. When the couple divorced, Muhammad married Zaynab. It was the legitimacy of this marriage that is authorized by the Qur'an. The convoluted arguments of the classical scholars as well as modern writers cannot take us beyond the simple facts. It was a subject of controversy in Muhammad's time as it remains today.

What is more significant is that all of Muhammad's wives except Aisha had been married before. This would have been a considerable change in a society in which virginity on marriage was a significant badge of status.

Moreover, Muhammad appreciated and respected his wives as independent women, women who were helpers and supporters in his mission. There is no trace of misogyny in his treatment of his wives, or women in general. Born into a society in which female infanticide was practised, Muhammad proclaimed that those who loved their daughters and did not prefer their male child to her shall enter Paradise. He is also reported to have said that if one wanted to know the character of a man one should enquire about the condition of his wife!

How beautiful?

There is much discussion in the classical sources about the beauty of Muhammad's wives. It is difficult to assess whether this was purely conventional or a detail serially embellished by later sources as something befitting the status of the Prophet. One suspects that the classical sources are telling us more about the outlook and attitudes of the writers than how it was in Medina. But there is no doubt that Muhammad himself enjoyed the company of women and a robust sex life.

And his wives were not mere trophies. They were independent minded and played a significant part in the political life of the Muslim community after the Prophet's death. All who had converted to Islam before the hijra – Sawdah, Hafsah, Zaynab, Umm Salama, Umm Habiba – must have had strength of character and determination. Hafsah was not only feisty but also literate and became the custodian of the original compilation of the Qur'an on which Uthman's authoritative text is based. Zaynab was renowned for her work amongst the destitute and earned the nickname of 'Mother of the Poor' for her generosity and charity. Umm Salama is credited with providing the strategy that helped Muhammad quell the dissension among his followers over the concessions he made in the Treaty of Hudaibiya. Most independent and forthright of them all was Aisha, the child bride who grew up in Muhammad's household. She became a major figure in the political battles of the early Muslim community and, by virtue of her close relationship with the Prophet, a principal source of information about his life, character and actions, the very foundation of the reports that became hadith. Thus, his wives were the prototype of the new social compact Muhammad was seeking to create in which women were encouraged to come forward as active participants in society, as friends and helpers alongside their menfolk. It is clear that Muhammad valued their advice and contribution to his mission.

Tracing the rationale behind Muhammad's marriages or his battles does not alter or apologize for the basic facts. However, the details are an essential part of forming a reasoned opinion on the subject. Muhammad was a man of his time, shaped by the conventions and traditions of the world into which he was born. Within such a context he was clearly an enlightened man who sought radical change to set his society on a better moral and ethical path.

11

The man and his character

ALL THAT
MATTERS

<u>Throughout his life Muhammad's most insistent self-description was 'I am a man like you.'</u>

He was a man of integrity, with an innate modesty and warm personality. Despite being the centre of attention, the inescapable person of renown, he was devoid of all forms of pomposity or snobbery. Khadija's servant, Maysara, who accompanied Muhammad on the trading mission to Syria, gave a glowing report not just of his conduct of business but also of how well he had treated him, a human detail that stands behind the more elaborate signs and portents that Maysara is said to have reported. And the same characteristic is found in the words of Anas bin Malik, Muhammad's servant much later in his life: 'He served me more than I served him. He was never angry with me. He never treated me badly.'[39] And Muhammad himself said, 'The dearest one in a society is the one who always serves others'. If someone sent a servant to summon Muhammad he would follow behind rather than assume a dominant position insistent on leading the way; most often, he would walk hand in hand with the servant. This characteristic of humility and respect for others can be seen in Muhammad as a husband and father, friend, social reformer and community builder.

Respect and dignity was something to be given to everyone irrespective of their status, and this is a consistent theme running through Muhammad's life. When he met people he gave them his complete attention, turning his whole body to address them and clasping their hands affectionately so that it was said that he was never the first to withdraw from a handshake. His most striking feature, much commented on by all his contemporaries, was the glow that lit up his face.

The Prophet's passions

Muhammad had two great passions: dates and perfume. He would rub musk and perfumes on his face, head and hands, and he frequently used aloe wood oil and camphor on his body and clothes.

Muhammad was a man who had known misfortune and suffering and retained sympathy and compassion for the needs of others throughout his life. And in this he has aptly been described as a living sermon on the moral core of the Qur'an: the need to establish social justice and equity as the basis of societal and human relations.

When he became the acknowledged leader of Medina, Muhammad continued to live a modest and frugal life.

He lived in a compound around the mosque in Medina. There were no guards at the gates of his humble home. He wore simple clothes, declining to wear silk or gold. Indeed he demonstrated a horror of opulence, display and their inherent dangers. He associated gold inextricably with pride and the cruelty of royal courts. He had a keen awareness of such temptations: 'it is not poverty that I fear', he said about Muslims, 'but the worldly riches given to you as they were given to those who had gone before you and you begin to vie with one another for them as they vied for them, and they may destroy you as they destroyed them'.[40] Rather than embracing the status symbols and trappings of a ruler, Muhammad assisted in the routine household chores. When the community set to work digging the defensive trench around Medina, Muhammad joined in. Refugees or persons in need were never turned away. Even when he and his family had little for themselves, whoever turned up would receive shelter and a share of what was available. 'Feed the hungry' was his constant mantra. Although he lived in a society in which racial pride was endemic, there is no trace of it in Muhammad's outlook. His farewell sermon

▲ The Sacred Mosque, with the Kaaba, expanded and modernized

underlined this principle in the ringing declaration that there was no preference for an Arab over a non-Arab.

Muhammad was clearly a man who formed strong and enduring relationships. His foster mother Halima was not considered a hired wet nurse; she remained a cherished part of his life and was feasted and cared for whenever she visited Mecca. Indeed, in a time of drought and famine, his wife Khadija presented Halima with a camel and 40 sheep, the means to rebuild the livelihood of a Bedouin family. He was deeply fond of his friend and constant companion, Abu Bakr, with whom he established a lifelong relationship.

A prophet is a person driven by spirituality, yet this never displaced Muhammad's practicality nor his gentle self-deprecating sense of humour. However much he commended prayer to his followers, one of his famous aphorisms is 'Pray – and tie your camel.' It is the upshot of a story about a man so intent on praying that he forgot to hobble his camel. For Muhammad, prayer was a means to become more aware of earthly realities and practicalities rather than a substitute for them.

He simply did not allow people to make him into a prodigy. He claimed no infallibility and moved swiftly to contradict any attempts to ascribe to him knowledge he did not possess. A familiar story illustrates this point. It happened when Muhammad was passing by a date orchard. The farmer was pollinating his crop and interpreted a comment by Muhammad to mean that this practice was somehow improper. When he learned of this, Muhammad immediately denounced the idea, saying he had no specialized knowledge and on such practical matters one should defer only to those with expertise. He was a man who, despite having no formal learning, had the highest regard for learning, as exemplified in his numerous sayings on the subject: 'Go in quest of knowledge even unto China'; 'An hour's contemplation is better than a year's adoration'; 'One learned man is harder on the devil than a thousand ignorant worshippers'; 'The ink of the scholar is more holy than the blood of the martyr'; and 'He who leaves home in search of knowledge walks in the path of God'.[41]

As insistently as he denied infallible knowledge in practical matters, Muhammad rejected any suggestion that portents or supernatural signs were associated with him or events in his life. When an eclipse occurred at the time of the death of his infant son and people described it as heaven weeping for his misfortune, Muhammad declared it was only a natural phenomenon. However extraordinary a prophet and messenger of God might seem to other people, keeping a firm hold on normality was central to Muhammad's character and attitude.

Muhammad became the leader of a community, not its ruler. Muslims were asked to make decisions in consultation and by consensus. The mosque in Medina was where the community came together to determine policy. Muhammad participated in these discussions and was ready to be counselled and contradicted by anyone with a sound argument. It is recorded that this even included being upbraided by one old woman and Muhammad agreeing with her.

Integrity meant that while Muhammad made no exaggerated claims for himself he would not allow others to provide them for him. When his beloved uncle, Abu Talib, was dying and declined embracing Islam, Muhammad was told by a person who heard his last dying words that Abu Talib had indeed made the declaration of faith. Muhammad simply replied: 'I did not hear it.' Even in such circumstances when it must have been his dearest personal wish and one easily accomplished, Muhammad stood firm. He would not claim nor allow the report of something he did not know to be true.

The message Muhammad proclaimed was that on the Day of Judgement wealth, fame, lineage, position in society, friendship with poets, the beauty of women in one's household and the number of one's descendants, the value system of the world he was born into, would make no difference. It is by the precepts of this message that he lived, giving emphasis to what he considered most important: feeding the poor, caring for orphans, sheltering widows and protecting the weak. He was a man who proclaimed the compassion and mercy of a forgiving God, and in his judgements and decisions there is clear evidence that he preferred and strove to err on the side of forgiveness.

Cat lover

Muhammad adored cats. Once he cut a hole in a robe he was wearing so that he could remove a sleeping cat without disturbing it.

Just 50 years after his death, Muhammad's followers could be found in Persia and Egypt and were on their way to Spain. Within a century, Islam would become a global religion and civilization. It was the emulation of Muhammad's virtues by his followers that took Islam to the zenith of civilization, and it was the neglect of these virtues that eventually led to the decline and fall of Muslim civilization.

Muhammad's qualities are not personified by how he cleaned his teeth, washed for prayer, the length of his beard or his appearance – the kind of detail that contemporary Muslims try to emulate. Rather, it is the man's character and personality that have something to teach us all, whether we are believers or not.

His emphasis on social justice, equality, mercy and compassion in human relationships has lessons for everyone. His life demonstrates the transformative potential of individuals and society. The pursuit of basic virtues, Muhammad tells us, can change everyone for the better.

5 classical biographies

1   Ibn Ishaq's *Life of Muhammad*

Muhammad ibn Ishaq (d. 767/8), born in Medina, was a historian and collector of the traditions of the Prophet, which formed the basis of his biography. Written over 100 years after the death of the Prophet, it was later edited by his student, Abdul Malik ibn Hashm (d. 833) – it is ibn Hashm's version that has survived. Full of poems (most of which ibn Hashm tried to edit out) and evocative descriptions, it is considered to be the most authentic and authoritative biography of the Prophet.

Ibn Ishaq, *Life of Muhammad*, trans. A Guillaume (Oxford: Oxford University Press, 1955)

2   Al-Waqidi's *Life of Muhammad*

Abu Abdullah Muhammad Ibn Omar Ibn Waqid (748–822) was born in Medina and thrived during the time of the legendry Abbasid Caliph, Harun al-Rashid. A historian and a bibliophile (he had acquired a massive library), Al-Waqidi compiled his work about the same time as ibn Hashm was editing ibn Ishaq's biography. The work consists largely of the battles and expeditions of the Prophet Muhammad. Later scholars, such as ibn Khaldun, the fourteenth-century historian and founder of sociology, attacked al-Waqidi for not being rigorous.

The Life of Muhammad: Al-Waqidi's Kitab al-Maghazi, ed. R Faizer, trans. R Faizer, A Ismail and A K Tayob (London: Routledge, 2011)

3   Ibn Sa'd's *The Book of Major Classes*

Muhammad ibn Sa'd (784–845), born in Basra, Iraq, was a biographer and a scribe. He is regarded as a major authority on biographical literature of the first century of Islam. The first two volumes of *The Book of Major Classes*, a compendium of biographical information on the major personalities, are devoted to the biography of the Prophet. Traditions of the Prophet are used throughout to knit an overall narrative.

Ibn Sa'd, *Kitab Al-Tabaqat Al-Kabir*, trans. S Moinul Haq (Delhi: Kitab Bhavan, two volumes, 2009)

4   *The History of al-Tabari*

Abu Ja'far Muhammad ibn Jarir al-Tabari (838–923), born in the Iranian city of Amol, was among the first and most influential historians of Islam. *The History of Prophets and Kings*, more commonly known as *The History of al-Tabari*, is a work of universal history, consisting of 40 volumes and covering the period from the creation of the world to 915. Volumes 4–9 are devoted to the life of the Prophet Muhammad. Tabari was interested only in gathering everything, whatever its merit, in one place, and left critical sifting to others.

Ehsan Yar-Shater, ed., *The History of al-Tabari* (New York: State University of New York Press, 40 vols, published between 1989 and 2007).

5   Ibn Kathir, *The Life of the Prophet Muhammad*

Abu Al-Fida 'Imad Ad-Din Isma'il bin 'Umar bin Kathir (1301–73), born in Damascus, was a historian, jurist and collector of the traditions of the Prophet. Like ibn Ishaq's biography, ibn Kathir's work was later edited. Rather than a narrative biography, it is a collection of the sayings of the Prophet giving accounts of various incidents in his life.

Ibn Kathir, *The Life of the Prophet Muhammad* (Al-Sira al-Nabawiyya, trans. T Le Gassick (London: Garnet, three volumes, 1998)

10 canonical collections of traditions

The traditions of the Prophet Muhammad, known as hadith, are the records of his sayings, discourses, practices and way of life. Collected around 200 years after the death of Muhammad, the hadith serve as the second, after the Qur'an, most important source of guidance for Muslims. There are six major collections, called *Al-Sihah al-Sittah*, or 'the authentic six'. In order of authenticity they are:

6   *Sahih Bukhari* by Imam Bukhari (810–70), who, as his name suggests, was born in Bukhara, now in Uzbekistan. He is said to have collected over 600,000 hadith, but regarded only 7,275 as authentic, rejecting the rest as untrustworthy. *Sahih Bukhari* is divided into 97 books, covering subjects such as faith, worship and knowledge, marriage and divorce, food and drink, Jihad, and the Prophet's career in Medina.

7   *Sahih Muslim* by Imam Muslim (821–75), who was born in Nishapur in northeastern Iran. He selected 9,200 hadith from a total of 300,000 that he collected as authentic. *Sahih Muslim* is better organised than *Sahih Bukhari*, with different versions of a tradition grouped together in the same place.

8   *Sunan al-Sughra* by al-Nasai (829–915), who was born in the city of Nasa in western Asia. His collection is said to be politically biased towards Ali, the fourth Caliph and the cousin of the Prophet Muhammad.

9 *Sunan Abu Dawood* (d. 889), who was born in Sistan, in eastern Iran. He is said to have collected 500,000 hadith over a 20-year period, but regarded only 4,600 as authentic. His collection is seen as controversial, with classical scholars questioning the authenticity of a number of hadith he labelled as authentic.

10 *Jami al-Trimidhi* by al-Tirmidhi (824–92), who was born in Termez, now in Uzbekistan. His collection includes a commentary on the Qur'an.

11 *Sanun ibn Majah* by ibn Majah (824–87), who was born in Qazwin, Iran. The collection contains 4,000 hadith organized in 32 books. *Sanun ibn Majahi* is also rather controversial as some of its hadith were later declared to be forgeries.

In general, Sunni Muslims use only *Sahih Bukhari* and *Sahih Muslim*, and regard them as the most authentic. Together, they contain 7,000 hadith, excluding repetitions.

Shia Muslims have their own four books of hadith:

12 *Kitab al-Kafi* by Kulayni (864–941), who is said to have been born somewhere between Tehran and Qom in Iran. The collection is divided into three sections and contains over 15,000 narrations, but many are regarded by Shia scholars as inauthentic.

13 *Man la Yahdhuruhu'l Faqih* of Shaikh Saduq (d. 991), who was probably born in Iran. The title of the collection translates as 'Every man is his own lawyer'; quite naturally, its emphasis is on legal subjects.

14 *Tahdhib al-Ahkam* by Abu Ja'far al-Tusi (995–1067), who was born in Tus, Iran, and is regarded as one of the most influential thinkers of Shia Islam. This collection is exclusively devoted to aspects of the Sharia, or Islamic law.

15 *Al-Istibsar* by Abu Ja'far al-Tusi (995–1067). This collection contains 5,511 hadith, and focuses on Islamic jurisprudence.

10 popular biographies

16 Martin Lings, *Muhammad: His Life Based on Early Sources* (London: Allen and Unwin, 1983)

The most widely read among Muslims. Lings retells the story of the Prophet Muhammad using ibn Ishaq, ibn Sa'd, Tabari and other classical sources. But the work has been criticized for too heavy a reliance on Waqidi, who is seen by some as lacking in objectivity and rigour.

17 Muhammad Husayn Haykal, *The Life of Muhammad*, trans. I Ragi al-Faruqi (Indianapolis, IN: North American Trust Publication, 1976)

Originally published in 1933, this is one of the most influential biographies of recent times. Haykal (1888–1956), an Egyptian writer, journalist and politician, was concerned with debunking the works of Western scholars and becomes apologetic in places. But it is a well-researched biography that attempts to show the relevance of Muhammad to modern life.

18 Shibli Numani, *Sirat un Nabi*, trans. M Tayyib Bakhsh Budayuni (Lahore: Kazi Publications, two volumes, 1979)

Regarded as one of the best works on Muhammad in Urdu, Numani (1857–1914), a highly respected scholar who flourished during the Raj, conceived it as a comprehensive six-volume study. But he managed to complete only two volumes before his death. The project was completed by his student, Sayyed Sulaiman Nadvi (1884–1953). Widely read in the original, the translation is poor and does not do justice to Numani's brilliant prose.

19 Abul Hasan Ali Nadwi, *Muhammad Rasulullah: The Life of Prophet Muhammad*, trans. M Ahmad (Lucknow: Islamic Research and Publications, 1978)

Nadwi (1913–99) was a superstar among Indian religious scholars. His unmatched command of Arabic made him very popular in the Middle East. *Muhammad Rasulullahi* was originally written in Arabic, but this is a translation of an Urdu translation. Nadwi's concerns are with authenticity and accuracy.

20 W Montgomery Watt, *Muhammad: Prophet and Statesman* (Oxford: Oxford University Press, 1961)

A scholarly analysis, exploring the social and political background of Muhammad's Arabia, his political achievements and the influence of Judaism and Christianity on shaping Islam.

21 Abdul Hameed Siddiqui, *The Life of Muhammad* (Lahore: Islamic Publications, 1969)

A devotional portrait, popular with Muslims from the Indian subcontinent.

22 Karen Armstrong, *Muhammad: Prophet of Our Time* (London: Atlas Books, 2006)

A beautifully written, balanced and illuminating portrait.

23 Barnaby Rogerson, *The Prophet Muhammad: A Biography* (London: Little Brown, 2003)

Takes the reader to seventh-century Arabia and makes him feel as though he is there.

24 Ziauddin Sardar, *Muhammad: Aspects of a Biography* (Leicester: Islamic Foundation, 1978)

Written as a novella and popular with young Muslims.

25 Eliot Weinberger, *Muhammad* (London: Verso, 2006)

A lyrical prose poem on the spiritual aspects of Muhammad's life.

10 scholarly texts

26 Marshall G S Hodgson, *The Venture of Islam* (Chicago: Chicago University Press, three volumes, 1974)

A magisterial work that explores how the teachings of Muhammad produce a global civilization. Book 1 of Volume 1 looks at Muhammad, the challenges he faced, and how the early Muslim state was formed.

27 M M Azami, *Studies in Early Hadith Literature* (Indianapolis: American Trust Publication, 1978)

A detailed examination of the authenticity of hadith, which also looks at early texts. Considered as a key text by some Muslim scholars.

28 F E Peters, *Muhammad and the Origins of Islam* (New York: State University of New York Press, 1994)

A critical and sometimes cynical reading of ibn Ishaq's *Life of Muhammad*.

29 Mohammad Hashim Kamali, *Hadith Methodology* (Selangor: Ilmiah Publishers, 2002)

A wide-ranging discussion of the authenticity, compilation, classification and criticism of hadith, which offers a string of proposals for reform.

30 Carl W Ernest, *Following Muhammad* (Chapel Hill, NC: University of North Carolina Press, 2003)

Subtitled 'Rethinking Islam in the contemporary world', Ernest explains how the teachings of Muhammad can be best followed in the twenty-first century.

31 Irving M Zeitlin, *The Historical Muhammad* (Oxford: Polity Press, 2007)

Examines scholarly claims and counterclaims, including more recent scholarship, about crucial aspects of Muhammad's life – such as objections to the Islamic theory of Abraham, the Prophet and the Jewish tribes of Medina, and the role of Christianity in the origins of Islam.

32 M Hamidullah, *The Life and Work of the Prophet of Islam* (New Delhi: Adam Publishers, 2007)

Originally published in 1959, this is a detailed scholarly examination of Muhammad's life based on documentary evidence.

33 Jonathan A C Brown, *Hadith: Muhammad's Legacy in the Medieval and Modern World* (London: OneWorld, 2009)

A detailed examination of Muslim scholarship of hadith throughout history. An engaging and important work.

34 Fred M Donner, *Muhammad and the Believers* (Cambridge, MA: Harvard University Press, 2010)

Critically examines the traditional accounts of the life of Muhammad and argues that the origins of Islam lie in the 'Community of Believers', which included Muslims, Christians and Jews in its early years and was begun by the Prophet Muhammad.

35 George Schoeler, *The Biography of Muhammad: Nature and Authenticity* (London: Routledge, 2011)

Examines the early biographies of the Prophet, both written and oral modes of transmission, and concludes that we have no reason to doubt 'the *main outlines* of the reports' that emerged one or two generations after the death of the Prophet.

100 ideas

5 films about Muhammad

36 *The Message* (1976), written by H A L Craig, A B Jawdat al-Sahhar, Tawfiq al-Hakim, et al., produced and directed by Moustapha Akkad, Filmco International Productions

A brilliant, well-crafted historical epic chronicling the life and times of Muhammad. The Prophet, according to Islamic tradition, is not depicted, nor do we hear his voice. The presence of Muhammad in a particular scene is depicted by light organ music, and his words, as he spoke them, are repeated by other characters. The main characters of the film are Hamza (played by Anthony Quinn), the paternal uncle of Muhammad, with Abu Safyan and his wife Hind (played by Michael Ansara and Irene Papas) as the villains of the piece.

37 *Muhammad: The Last Prophet* (2004), written by Brian Nissen, directed by Richard Rich, produced by Badr International, Distributed by Fine Media Group

An enchanting, animated version of the life of Muhammad. As in *The Message*, Muhammad is not depicted; the character speaking to him faces the camera.

38 *Muhammad: Legacy of the Prophet* (2002), produced by Alex Kronemer and Michael Wolfe, PBS

A documentary that explores the life of Muhammad through both historical records and the stories of American Muslims.

39 *The Islam Collection*, History Channel, not dated

A two-disc set that looks at Islam in general and talks about Muhammad in tracing the origins of Islam.

40 *The Life of Muhammad* (2011), written by Ziauddin Sardar, produced and directed by Faris Kirmani, BBC

A highly acclaimed three-hour critical documentary, presented by Rageh Omar, exploring not just the life of Muhammad but also his historical context and how his teachings have been interpreted today.

10 websites

41 http://web.archive.org

An ideal place to download books on Muhammad, including ibn Ishaq's *Life of Muhammad* and Martin Lings's *Muhammad: His Life Based on Early Sources.*

42 www.bbc.co.uk/learningzone/clips/the-prophet-muhammad/

From the BBC, with videos and other material to use in the classroom.

43 www.iium.edu.my/deed/hadith/

A database of hadith, including *Sahih Bukhari* and *Sahih Muslim*.

44 www.muhammad.net

'Biography, mission and message of Muhammad', with many sermons, prayers and devotional material.

45 www.prophetmuhammadforall.org

A multilingual site that provides a general background to the life of Muhammad and small collections of hadith and devotional music to download, as well as a couple of contemporary biographies.

46 www.rasoulallah.net

A multilingual devotional site.

47 www.amaana.org/prophet/prophetmuhammad.htm

The Islamaili takes on the Prophet, with many pieces of devotional music to download.

48 www.al-islam.org/lifeprophet/

A site that promotes the views of Tablighi Jamaat, a worldwide evangelical organization.

49 www.kalamullah.com/muhammad.html

A database of devotional resources, including many contemporary biographies.

50 http://rsulallah.wordpress.com/

A site containing the Saudi Wahhabi sect's views on Muhammad.

50 sayings of Muhammad

51 God Almighty is good and loves goodness, is pure and loves purity.

52 God does not look upon your bodies and appearances. He looks upon your heart and your deeds.

53 The world is green and beautiful and God has appointed you His stewards over it.

54 The whole earth is created a place of worship, pure and clean.

55 The whole of creation is God's family.

56 Purity is half the faith.

57 If a Muslim plants a tree or sows a field and men and beasts and birds eat from it, all of it is charity on his part.

58 Whosoever plants a tree and diligently looks after it until it matures and bears fruit is rewarded.

59 Whoever is kind to His creatures, God is kind to him.

60 The search for knowledge is a sacred duty imposed upon every Muslim.

61 Seek knowledge from the cradle to the grave.

62 Learn to know yourself.

63 An hour's contemplation is better than a year's prayer. To spend more time in learning is better than spending more time in praying. It is better to impart knowledge one hour in the night than to pray the whole night.

64 God has not created anything better than reason, or anything more perfect or more beautiful than reason.

65 Strive always to excel in virtue and truth.

66 Say what is true, even though it may be bitter and displeasing to people.

67 Little but sufficient is better than the abundant and the alluring.

68 Every religion has a special character and the characteristic of Islam is modesty.

69 Modesty and faith are joined together and if either of them is lost the other goes also.

70 Charity is incumbent upon every human limb every day upon which the sun rises. To bring about reconciliation between two contestants is charity. Helping a person to mount his animal or to load his baggage onto it is charity. A good word is charity. To move obstacles in the street is charity. Smiling upon the face of your brother is charity.

71 At evening, do not expect to live till morning. At morning, do not expect to live till evening. Take from your health for your illness, from your life for your death.

72 Rejoice. And hope for that which will please you.

73 It is not poverty which I fear for you but that you might begin to desire the world as others before you desired it and it might destroy you as it destroyed them.

74 Riches are pleasant and sweet for him who acquires them by the [good] way. They are a source of blessing. But they are not blessed for him who seeks them out of greed. He is like the one who eats and is not filled.

75 Hasten to do good before you are overtaken by perplexing adversity, corrupting prosperity, disabling disease, babbling dotage and sudden death.

76 Safeguard yourselves against miserliness for it ruined those who were before you.

77 Beware of envy for envy devours good works as fire devours fuel.

78 Righteousness is about that which the soul feels tranquil.

79 Wrongdoing is that which wavers the soul and moves to and fro in the breast even though the people have given you their legal opinion in its favour.

80 Good character melts away mistakes just as water melts away ice. Bad character spoils deeds just as vinegar spoils honey.

81 Make things easy and do not make them hard; and cheer people up and do not rebuff them.

82 Gentleness adorns everything; and its absence leaves everything tainted.

83 The rights of women are sacred.

84 He who is not compassionate to our little ones and does not acknowledge the honour due to our elders is not one of us.

85 He is not a believer who eats his fill while his neighbour remains hungry by his side.

86 He will not enter paradise whose neighbour is not secure from his mischief.

87 You should be humble. Let no one boast over his neighbour; and let no one oppress his neighbour also.

88 If a person loves his brother, he should tell him so.

89 If one of you sees something reprehensible, he should change it with his hand; and if he is not capable of that then with his tongue; and if he is not capable of that then he should detest it with his heart but that shows the weakest of faith.

90 Indecency disfigures everything; modesty enhances the charm of everything.

91 As you are, so you will have rulers over you.

92 The most excellent of jihad is to speak the truth in the face of a tyrannical ruler.

93 The great jihad is the jihad of the heart (the conquest of the self).

94 Pay the worker before his sweat dries.

95 It is a sin for a person to hold back the due of one whose living he controls.

96 He who brings goods for sale is blessed with good fortune. But he who keeps them till the prices rise is accursed.

97 Feed the hungry and visit the sick.

98 Assist any person oppressed, Muslim or non-Muslim.

99 Humility and courtesy are acts of piety.

100 The value of the world in comparison to the Hereafter is like a droplet in the ocean.

Notes

1 Azami M M, *The History of the Qur'anic Text* (Leicester: UK Islamic Academy, 2003), p. 68.

2 Sardar Z, *Reading the Qur'an* (London: Hurt, 2011).

3 On the science of hadith criticism and the importance of hadith, see Brown J A C, *Hadith: Muhammad's Legacy in the Medieval and Modern World* (Oxford: OneWorld, 2009).

4 *Sahih Bukhari*, trans. M Asad (Gibraltar: Dar al-Andalus, 1981); there are numerous other translations.

5 *Sahih Muslim*, trans. A Hamid Siddiqui (Lahore: Islamic Book Service, three volumes, 2005).

6 ibn Ishaq, *The Life of Muhammad*, trans. A Guillaume (Oxford: Oxford University Press, 1955).

7 Al-Waqidi, *The Life of Muhammad*, trans. R Faizer et al. (London: Routledge, 2011).

8 Ibn Saad, *Kitab Al-tabaqat Al-kabir*, trans. S Moinal Haq and H K Ghazanfar (New Delhi: Kitab Bhava, 1986).

9 Al-Tabari, *The History of al-Tabari* (New York: State University of New York Press, 39 volumes, various translators, 1985–2007).

10 Musa A Y, *Hadith as Scripture* (New York: Palgrave Macmillan, 2008).

11 Guillaume A, Introduction to *The Life of Muhammad* by ibn Ishaq (Oxford: Oxford University Press, 1978), p. xxiv.

12 Schoeler G, *The Biography of Muhammad: Nature and Authenticity* (London: Routledge, 2011) examines these opinions and finds them seriously flawed.

13 Sardar Z, *Orientalism* (Milton Keynes: Open University Press, 1999).

14 Quoted in Hoyland R G, *Arabia and the Arabs: From the Bronze Age to the Coming of Islam* (London: Routledge, 2001), p. 8.

15 Crone P, *Meccan Trade and the Rise of Islam* (Princeton: Princeton University Press, 1987).

16 *Diodorus of Sicily* translated by C H Oldfather, Volume II (London: William Heinemann Ltd. and Cambridge, MA: Harvard University Press, 1935), p. 217.

17 Hogarth D G, *The Penetration of Arabia* (London: Alston Rivers Limited, 1905), p. 18.

18 Ramadan T, *The Messenger: The Meanings of the Life of Muhammad* (London: Penguin, 2007), p. 14.

19 Zeitlin I M, *The Historical Muhammad* (Oxford: Polity Press, 2007), pp. 50–62.

20 ibn Ishaq, op. cit., p. 119.

21 Haykal M H, *The Life of Muhammad* (Indianapolis, IN: North American Trust Publication, 1976), pp. 98–9.

22 ibn Ishaq, op. cit., p. 229.

23 See Hamidullah M, *The First Written Constitution in the World* (Lahore: Ashraf, 1970) and Lecker M, *The 'Constitution of Medina': Muhammad's First Legal Document* (Princeton, NJ: Darwin Press, 2004). I have used the 'Translation of the Text of the Constitution', given by Hamidullah in *The Prophet's Establishing A State and His Succession* (Delhi: Adam Publishers, 2007), pp. 65–74.

24 ibn Ishaq, op. cit., p. 453.

25 Ibid, p. 464.

26 Rogerson B, *The Prophet Muhammad: A Biography* (London: Little Brown, 2003), p. 167.

27 Ibn Ishaq, op. cit., p. 503.

28 Ibid, p. 504.

29 Ibid, p. 505.

30 *History of Al-Tabari*, volume 8, p. 104.

31 Ibid, p. 108.

32 ibn Ishaq, op. cit., p. 553.

33 Ibid, p. 553.

34 There are a number of versions of the Farewell Sermon. I have summarized the one from ibn Ishaq, op. cit., p. 651.

35 Muir W, *Mahomet and Islam* (London: Smith, Elder & Co, 1895).

36 On H Lemmens see Djait H, *Europe and Islam* (Berkeley, CA: University of California Press, 1985).

37 Voltaire, *Mahomet the Prophet or Fanaticism: A Tragedy in Five Acts*, trans. R L Myers, (New York: Frederick Ungar, 1964), original 1736.

38 Count C F Volney, *The Ruins* (London and New York: Twentieth Century Publishing, 1882).

39 Quoted in Rogerson B, *The Prophet Muhammad: A Biography* (London: Little Brown, 2003), p. 129.

40 *Sahih Muslim*, Book 42, number 7065.

41 *Mishkat al-Masabih*, trans. J Robson (Lahore: Ashraf, 1963), Book II, 'Knowledge', pp. 50–63).

Select bibliography

Al-Tabari, *The History of al-Tabari* (New York: State University of New York Press, 1988), volumes vi–ix, various translators.

Al-Waqidi, *The Life of Muhammad*, trans. R Faizer et al. (London: Routledge, 2011).

Armstrong K, *Muhammad: Prophet of Our Time* (Atlas Books, 2006).

Azmi M M, *Studies in Early Hadith Literature* (Indianapolis, IN: American Trust Publications, 1978).

Brown J A C, *Hadith: Muhammad's Legacy in the Medieval and Modern World* (Oxford: OneWorld, 2009).

Brown J A C, *Muhammad: A Very Short Introduction* (Oxford: Oxford University Press, 2011).

Donner F M, *Muhammad and the Believers* (Cambridge, MA: Harvard University Press, 2010), pp. 58, 69.

Grunebaum G E, *Classical Islam: A History 600–1258*, (London: Allen and Unwin, 1970).

Hamidullah M, *The Battlefields of Prophet Muhammad* (Lahore: Ashraf, 1923).

Hamidullah M, *The First Written Constitution in the World* (Lahore: Ashraf, 1970).

Hamidullah M, *The Prophet's Establishing a State and His Succession* (New Delhi: Adam Publishers, 2007).

Hamidullah M, *The Life and Work of the Prophet of Islam* (New Delhi: Adam Publishers, 2007).

Haykal M H, *The Life of Muhammad* (Indianapolis, IN: North American Trust Publication, 1976).

Hodgson M, *The Venture of Islam* (Chicago, IL: Chicago University Press, 1974, 3 volumes).

Ibn Ishaq, *The Life of Muhammad*, trans. A Guillaume (Oxford: Oxford University Press, 1955).

Ibn Saad, *Kitab Al-tabaqat Al-kabir*, trans. S Moinal Haq and H K Ghazanfar (New Delhi: Kitab Bhava, 1986).

Kamali M H, *Hadith Methodology* (Kuala Lumpur: Ilmiah, 2002).

Lecker M, *The 'Constitution of Medina': Muhammad's First Legal Document* (Princeton, NJ: Darwin Press, 2004).

Lings M, *Muhammad: His Life Based on Early Sources* (London: Allen and Unwin, 1983).

Musa A Y, *Hadith as Scripture* (London: Palgrave, 2008).

Peters F E, *Muhammad and the Origins of Islam* (New York: State University of New York Press, 1994).

Rahman F, *Islam and Modernity: Transformation of an Intellectual Tradition* (Chicago, IL: Chicago University Press, 1982).

Rogerson B, *The Prophet Muhammad: A Biography* (London: Little Brown, 2003).

Sahih Bukhari, trans. Muhammad Asad (Gibraltar: Dar al-Andalus, 1981).

Sardar Z, *Muhammad: Aspects of A Biography* (Leicester: Islamic Foundation, 1978).

Sardar Z, *Desperately Seeking Paradise* (London: Granta, 2004).

Sardar Z, *Reading the Qur'an* (London: Hurst, 2011).

Schoeler G, *The Biography of Muhammad: Nature and Authenticity* (London: Routledge, 2011).

Watt W M, *Muhammad at Mecca* (Oxford: Oxford University Press, 1953).

Watt W M, *Muhammad at Medina* (Oxford: Oxford University Press, 1991).

Watt W M, *Muhammad: Prophet and Statesman* (Oxford: Oxford University Press, 1961).

Weinberger E, *Muhammad* (London: Verso, 2006).

Zeitlin I M, *The Historical Muhammad* (Oxford: Polity Press, 2007).

Index

ALL THAT MATTERS: MUHAMMAD